Peterson's SAT Preparation Course Lesson Book

Custom Course

THOMSON

PETERSON'S™

Australia • Canada • Mexico • Singapore • Spain • United Kingdom • United States

About Thomson Peterson's

Thomson Peterson's (www.petersons.com) is a leading provider of education information and advice with books and online resources focusing on education search, test preparation, and financial aid. Its Web site offers searchable databases and interactive tools for contacting educational institutions, online practice tests and instruction, and planning tools for securing financial aid. Peterson's serves 110 million education customers annually.

For more information, contact Peterson's, 2000 Lenox Drive, Lawrenceville, NJ 08648; 800-338-3282; or find us on the World Wide Web at www.petersons.com/about.

ISBN: 0-7869-2048-5

Printed in the United States of America

10 9 8 7 6 5 4 3 2 1   07 06 05

Contents

Session 1: About the SAT

In this unit, you will learn to:

- identify the nature and function of the SAT.

- describe the structure and format of the SAT.

- recognize what will and will not be tested on the SAT.

- identify the key components of successful SAT preparation.

What Is the SAT?

Why does the SAT Exist?

How does the SAT make the admissions process fairer?

_____

What is a standardized test?

Why is it good that the SAT is a standardized test?

_____

Is it an IQ Test?

What else do colleges consider in evaluating you as a candidate?

_____

Preparing for the SAT

To be fully prepared for the SAT, you must do five important things.

Know the Test

Know the Content

Know the Strategies

Keep Practicing

Visualize Success

What is your goal on the SAT? Write it here so that you can start to visualize it.

_____

_____

_____

Your SAT Course

Your SAT course has everything you need to do your best on the SAT.

Diagnostic:

Lessons:

Homework:

Practice test:

What do you need to do to make sure this course improves your score?

_____

_____

_____

SAT Structure

Knowing the structure of the SAT will save you time and keep you from getting disoriented on Test Day.

Topic	Sections	Time	Content	Question Types	Score Ranges
Math	3	Two 25-minute sections and one 20-minute section	Numbers and operations; algebra and functions; geometry; statistics, probability and data analysis	Multiple choice; Grid-Ins	200-800
Critical Reading	3	Two 25-minute sections and one 20-minute section	Critical reading and sentence-level reading	Sentence completions; short-passage reading; long-passage reading	200-800
Writing	3	Two 25-minute sections and one 10-minute section	Grammar, usage, word choice, writing	Identifying sentence errors; improving sentences; improving paragraphs; student-written essay	200-800
Unscored	1	One 25-minute section	Could be any topic	Could be any topic	No score
Total	10	3 hours and 45 minutes			600-2400

Note: The experimental section (sometimes called the equating section) does not count toward your score.

SAT Questions

The SAT content is similar to what you learn in high school. You won't need to learn a whole new set of skills before taking the SAT.

The SAT tests general skills, such as how to:

- read critically.
- write effectively.
- solve problems.

Your Turn

1. Three things I can do (besides taking this course) to prepare for the SAT are:

_____

_____

_____

SAT Question Difficulty

Most questions on the SAT get harder as you move along. The exceptions are the Reading Comprehension questions and the Essay. Reading Comprehension questions do not necessarily appear in order of difficulty, and the Essay contains one question that you answer by composing a written response.

You get the same number of points for easy questions as you do for hard questions, so make sure to go for the easy points at the beginning of each section before tackling the tougher ones at the end.

Your Turn

2. An obvious-looking answer early in a set is _____.

3. An obvious-looking answer midway in a set is _____.

4. An obvious-looking answer late in a set is _____.

SAT Scoring

Your SAT score is actually several scores.

Raw Score

Your raw score is the total number of questions you answered correctly minus a wrong answer penalty for questions you answered incorrectly. You gain one point for every correct answer and lose a quarter of a point for every incorrect answer. The wrong answer penalty applies to all question types except Grid-Ins and the Essay. You get separate raw scores for Critical Reading, Writing, and Math.

Scaled Score

Raw scores are converted into scaled scores through a statistical process. You get scaled scores for Critical Reading, Math, and Writing. Each scaled score falls between 200 and 800. These three scaled scores make up your combined score, which ranges from 600 to 2400.

Percentile Score

The percentile score tells you how well you did in relation to other people who took the test. The percentile number reminds you that you are competing directly against other test takers.

Raw versus Scaled?

Small variations in your raw score can lead to a big leap in your scaled score.

Should I Guess?

Because there is a wrong-answer penalty for multiple-choice questions, you should never guess blindly on them. But if you can eliminate any of the wrong answer choices, it's worthwhile to guess.

On what question type should you always guess, even if you have no idea of the answer?

Three Ways to Raise Your Score

You can raise your score in three ways:

Correctly answer questions that you currently don't answer.

Correctly answer questions that you currently get wrong.

Most errors occur because you:

-
-
-

Answer fewer questions that you currently get wrong.

Thinking about your Diagnostic test, which of these three areas do you think you need to spend the most time improving?

_____

_____

SAT Registration

The SAT is administered seven times a year. Many students take the test in May or June, but another test date might be best for you.

Online

To register for the SAT online, go to www.collegeboard.com.

Mail

To register by mail, you will need what the College Board calls a "Registration Bulletin." You can get one in your school guidance counselor's office.

Phone

You can register for the SAT by phone only if you have registered for the SAT in the past. To register by phone, call 1-800-SAT-SCORE (toll-free) or 1-609-771-7600 (New Jersey), 24 hours a day, 7 days a week.

Fax

SAT registration by fax is available only for international test takers. If this is you, the fax form is included in the Registration Bulletin. Allow 3-5 days for the College Board to process your fax.

Additional fees apply for late registration and changing your testing date. To avoid a late fee, you must register at least:

_____

Some fee waivers are available for students who demonstrate economic need. If you need information about a fee waiver, you should:

_____

Note: Photocopying any part of this book is prohibited by law.

9

Summary

In this unit, you learned that:

- the nature of a standardized test is to be stable and predictable.

- except for Reading Comprehension and the Essay, SAT questions increase in difficulty as you progress through a section.

- a few extra points in your raw score can improve your scaled score.

- you can raise your score in three ways: answer more questions right that you were skipping, answer more questions right that you were answering wrong, and answer fewer questions that you were answering wrong.

- you must register in advance to take the SAT.

Session 2: Math Pacing

In this unit, you will learn to:

- raise your score by answering fewer questions.

- set sensible score goals for yourself.

- determine how many questions to answer to meet your score goals.

- choose which questions to answer to maximize your points.

- figure out why easy questions are easy and hard questions are hard.

- use the order of difficulty to help you answer questions.

Math Section Overview

There are:

- two 25-minute sections
- one 20-minute section

Math sections contain multiple-choice questions and Grid-Ins, which have no answer choices to choose from.

In each set, the problems are arranged in order of difficulty. The easier questions come first, then the medium questions, and finally the hardest questions.

What Is Pacing?

Pacing means focusing on the areas of the SAT where you'll earn the most points. Pacing is the best thing that you can do to improve your score. In other words, answering *fewer* questions can actually raise your score.

You should not answer every question on the SAT because:

_____

_____

20. If $a = \dfrac{3b^2}{c^3}$, then what happens to the value of a when b and c are doubled in value?

   (A) The value of a is quartered.
   (B) The value of a is halved.
   (C) The value of a is unchanged.
   (D) The value of a is doubled.
   (E) The value of a is tripled.

Should you spend your time on this question?

How to Choose a Score Goal

This table tells you how many questions you need to answer correctly for a variety of scores. Based on your score goals, you can figure out how many questions you should answer.

Score Goal	Raw Points Needed	Questions to Answer
350	7	11
400	12	16
450	18	23
500	25	31
550	30	37
600	38	46
650	43	52

Write your Diagnostic score here:

Math: _____

Write your score goal here:

Math: _____

How many questions should you attempt in order to reach your score goal?

_____

Tougher As You Go

How should you approach the easier questions in a Math section?

_____

_____

_____

How should you approach the medium questions in a Math section?

_____

_____

_____

How should you approach the hardest questions in a Math section?

_____

_____

_____

Easy or Hard?

3. What is 75% of 8?

(A) 4
(B) 5
(C) 6
(D) 8
(E) 9

9. What percent of 80 is 48?

(A) 50
(B) 60
(C) 65
(D) 70
(E) 75

12. 18 is 12% of what number?

(A) 75
(B) 97
(C) 120
(D) 150
(E) 225

19. If $2m + 3n$ equals 150% of $4n$, what is the value of $\dfrac{n}{m}$?

(A) $\dfrac{1}{6}$

(B) $\dfrac{1}{3}$

(C) $\dfrac{1}{2}$

(C) $\dfrac{2}{3}$

(D) 1

(E) $\dfrac{3}{2}$

Note: Photocopying any part of this book is prohibited by law.

15

How to Tell if You Should Move On

On the SAT, questions fall into one of three categories:

- questions you know you can solve
- questions you know you have no chance of solving
- questions you're not sure about

Questions You Know You Can Solve

These questions need no explanation. You simply answer them and move on. Check your math, but don't second-guess yourself.

Questions You Know You Have No Chance of Solving

If you have no idea how to approach a question, what the answer choices mean, or where to even begin guessing, skip it and move on. Save your energy for questions that will earn you points.

Questions You're Not Sure About

These are the tricky questions. Here are the things to keep in mind when deciding how long to spend on a question you're not sure about:

Where in the section it is because:

_____

What question type it is because:

_____

How much time you have left in the section because:

_____

The Two-Pass Method

The First Pass

- Do the early questions you know you can solve, skipping those that seem difficult.

- Note in the test booklet any question you skip so that you can go back to it later.

- Be careful to fill your next answer in the proper place on the answer sheet.

The Second Pass

- Stop your first pass when you get to the hard questions, and go back to the questions you skipped and try them again.

- If you make it through those questions and still have time left, see if any of the harder questions are in your areas of strength. However, do this only if you've spent enough time on the easy questions to be sure you got them right!

Hard Questions

If you follow the two-pass method and still have some time to work on hard questions, be very careful. Hard questions can be very tricky so you should focus on eliminating wrong answers.

17. The price of a DVD player was increased by 15%. Later it went on sale so the new price was decreased by 25%. The final price was what percent of the original price?

(A) 75%
(B) 85%
(C) 86.25%
(D) 87.5%
(E) 115%

Should You Guess?

Yes! We're going to show you how to make educated guesses that will earn you points, even when you don't completely understand the question. It is to your advantage to make educated guesses on the SAT, so guess aggressively.

Summary

In this unit, you learned that:

- you can raise your score by answering fewer questions.

- sensible score goals are 50-100 points higher than your Diagnostic scores.

- to maximize your score, answer questions earlier in a section, and those that you're likely to get right.

- you can use the score goal tables to figure out roughly how many questions you need to answer to meet your score goals.

- You can use the order of difficulty to help you answer questions.

Answer Key

20. B
 3. C
 9. B
12. D
19. C
17. C

Session 2: Math Question Types

In this unit, you will learn to:

- recognize the topics tested in the Math section of the SAT.

- understand the instructions to Problem Solving questions.

- use strategy to work through Roman numeral questions.

- grid in answers.

- use a calculator to increase your score.

- avoid common calculator errors.

Math Section Overview

Sections

There are three Math sections on the SAT:

- two 25-minute sections
- one 20-minute section

The 20-minute section and one 25-minute section consist entirely of multiple-choice questions. The other 25-minute section contains a mix of multiple-choice questions and Grid-Ins.

Topics

The Math section tests the following content areas:

- numbers and operations
- algebra and functions
- geometry
- statistics
- probability and data analysis

Score

You will receive a scaled score on the Math section of 200-800.

Why You Shouldn't Be Stressed

- Concepts are commonly taught by the 10th or 11th grade.
- It's the same for everyone.
- You can avoid hard questions if you want.
- Question with difficult concepts often have easy calculations.

Problem-Solving Instructions

STANDARD INSTRUCTIONS

Time—25 minutes	In this section solve each problem, using any available space on the page for scratchwork.
20 questions	Then decide which is the best of the choices given and fill in the corresponding oval on the answer sheet.

Note:
The use of a calculator is allowed. All numbers used are real numbers. Figures associated with problems in this test are meant to provide useful information to help solve the problems. They are always drawn to scale UNLESS it is stated in a problem that the figure is not drawn to scale. All figures lie in a plane unless otherwise specified.

1. Jackie owns three times as many fiction books as nonfiction books. If she owns a total of 48 books and all her books are either fiction or nonfiction, how many nonfiction books does she own?

(A) 12
(B) 16
(C) 24
(D) 32
(E) 36

Roman Numeral Questions

2. If x and y are integers and the product of x and y is a positive, even integer, which of the following must be true?

I. x and y are even
II. x and y are positive
III. x and y are prime

(A) None
(B) I only
(C) II only
(D) I and II only
(E) I, II, and III

3. A square has an area of 100. Which of the following could be the length of a straight line drawn completely within that square?

I. 8
II. 10
III. 14

(A) None
(B) I only
(C) II only
(D) I and II only
(E) I, II, and III only

Note: Photocopying any part of this book is prohibited by law.

22

Grid-In Directions

Because Grid-Ins require you to fill your answer into a funny-looking grid, the directions are extremely complicated. Don't worry about memorizing it all now. We'll make sure you understand them by the end of this lesson.

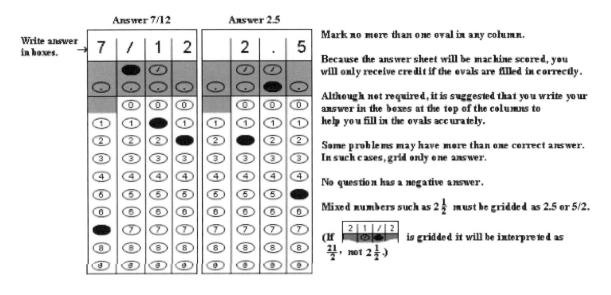

Mark no more than one oval in any column.

Because the answer sheet will be machine scored, you will only receive credit if the ovals are filled in correctly.

Although not required, it is suggested that you write your answer in the boxes at the top of the columns to help you fill in the ovals accurately.

Some problems may have more than one correct answer. In such cases, grid only one answer.

No question has a negative answer.

Mixed numbers such as $2\frac{1}{2}$ must be gridded as 2.5 or 5/2.

(If ⟨grid⟩ is gridded it will be interpreted as $\frac{21}{2}$, not $2\frac{1}{2}$.)

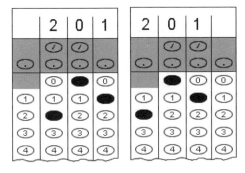

Answer = 201
Either position is correct

Note: You may start your answers in any column, space permitting. Columns not needed should be left blank.

Decimal Accuracy
If you obtain a decimal answer, enter the most accurate value that the grid will accommodate.
For example, if you obtain an answer such as 0.6666..., you should record the result as .666 or .667. Less accurate values such as .66 or .67 are not acceptable.

See below for acceptable ways to grid 2/3 = .6666...

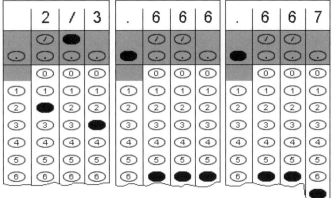

Grid Practice

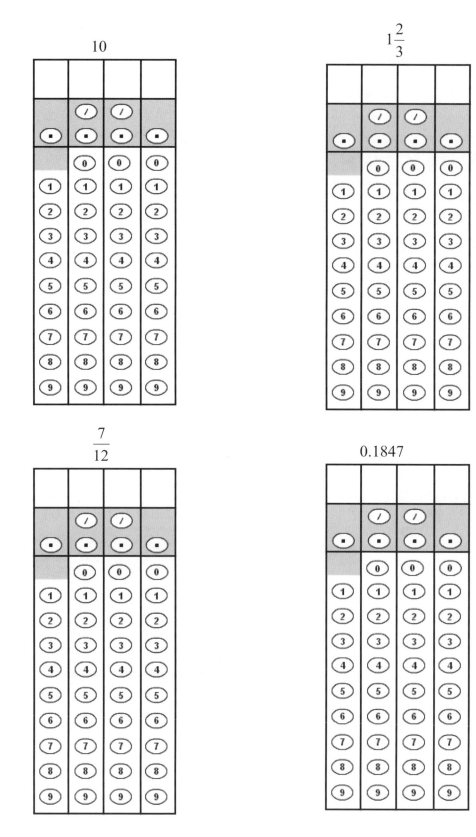

10

$1\frac{2}{3}$

$\frac{7}{12}$

0.1847

Ungriddable Numbers

- Mixed numbers cannot be gridded.

- The grid cannot accommodate negative numbers or values greater than 9,999.

Gridding Exercise

Decide whether each of the following numbers can be gridded in as it is, whether it needs to be converted before you can grid it in, or whether it can't be gridded at all (and you need to go back and recalculate your answer).

93

9,573

-1

3.4×10^3

3.4×10^5

$\sqrt{5}$

$\dfrac{23}{53}$

12,500

π

Note: Photocopying any part of this book is prohibited by law.

25

Grid-In Practice Questions

4. A farmer grows oranges and lemons only. His grove of 53 trees has 7 more orange trees than lemon trees. How many trees in the grove are lemon trees?

5. A shoe store sells only sneakers and boots. The ratio of sneakers to boots at that store is 8 : 3. What percent of the footwear at the store is boots? (Disregard the percent sign when gridding your answer.)

Note: Photocopying any part of this book is prohibited by law.

26

Calculator Strategy

Studies have shown that students who use a calculator on the SAT do slightly better than students who don't.

Most students who use a calculator still get fewer than half of the math questions right.

What Kind of Calculator Should You Bring?

- The best calculator to bring is one you know how to use.
- You don't need a fancy calculator.
- You can bring your scientific or graphing calculator and should do so if you are used to it.
- Install fresh batteries in your calculator the day before the test.

You will NOT be allowed to use:

- PDAs, such as a Palm Pilot
- laptops or portable computers
- calculators with typewriter-style keyboards
- calculators that make a great deal of noise
- calculators that have printers
- calculators that must be plugged in to electrical outlets

What's the bottom line about calculators on the SAT?

They won't solve the problems for you. In fact, getting too confident about having a calculator can actually hurt your score, because you won't spend enough time setting up the problem. Don't get overconfident and blow your score; think before you press any buttons.

Think Before You Press

Calculators are useful for:
- avoiding arithmetic mistakes.
- converting numbers that can't be gridded.

Don't abuse your calculator. Never start pressing buttons before you reach the end of the question.

6. The integer 80 is 25 percent of which of the following numbers?

(A) 10
(B) 20
(C) 25
(D) 160
(E) 320

What mistake do students make on the question above?

How to use a calculator on the SAT:

1. Read the question carefully.
2. Decide on the best way to solve the question.
3. Set up equations, if there are any.
4. Then, and only then, use your calculator

Calculator-Proof Questions

The SAT presents questions that can't easily be solved using a calculator.

7. If $x > 0$, which of the following fractions has the greatest value?

(A) $\dfrac{x}{2x+5}$

(B) $\dfrac{2x}{4x+11}$

(C) $\dfrac{3x}{6x+14}$

(D) $\dfrac{4x}{8x+19}$

(E) $\dfrac{5x}{10x+26}$

Two Laws of Calculators

There are two fundamental rules for using a calculator on the SAT:

1. Don't reach for your calculator until you've thought about the question.

2. If you need to punch a lot of numbers into your calculator to answer a question, think again; you are probably going about it the wrong way.

Punch this equation into your calculator:

$$3 + 8 \times 6 =$$

Did you get 66? Or 51?

Remember to Use PEMDAS!

P

E

M

D

A

S

8. If $y = 2 + \dfrac{x}{2}$ and $z = 3 + \dfrac{y}{3}$, what is the value of z when $x = 8$?

(A) $\dfrac{8}{3}$

(B) 3

(C) $\dfrac{11}{3}$

(D) 5

(E) $\dfrac{16}{3}$

Summary

In this unit, you learned that:

- you should understand the instructions for multiple-choice and Grid-In questions before you go into the test.

- you should grid in your answer in the simplest form.

- if you get an answer that can't be gridded, work the problem again.

- calculators only help you if you don't abuse them.

- there are certain situations in which your calculator can save you time.

Answer Key

1. A
2. A
3. E
4. 23
5. 27.2 or 27.3
6. E
7. C
8. D

Session 2: Critical Reading and Writing Pacing

In this unit, you will learn how to:

- raise your Critical Reading and Writing scores by answering fewer questions.

- set sensible score goals for yourself on Critical Reading and Writing.

- choose which questions to answer to maximize your points on Critical Reading and Writing.

- determine how many questions to answer to meet your score goals on Critical Reading and Writing.

- set pacing plans for yourself for Critical Reading and Writing.

What Is Pacing?

Pacing describes how you move through each section of the test, including:

- how many questions you answer
- how much time you spend on each question
- when and how you guess
- how much time you leave to check your work

For you, pacing means focusing on the areas of the SAT where you'll earn the most points.

What parts of the Critical Reading and Writing sections do you feel most confident about right now?

_____

_____

What parts of the Critical Reading and Writing sections do you feel least confident about right now?

_fill in the blanks_____

_____

Note: Photocopying any part of this book is prohibited by law.

32

The Importance of Pacing

Pacing—including answering fewer questions—is the best thing that you can do to improve your score.

The SAT is nearly 4 hours long. You will need to focus your energy where you will earn points, and not waste energy struggling over questions that you're unlikely to get correct.

You should not answer every Critical Reading and Writing question because:

for getting a question wrong you get points taken away

On some questions, fewer than 20% of test takers get the correct answer. Given how the SAT is scored, what does this tell you?

Don't guess questions

Note: Photocopying any part of this book is prohibited by law.

33

How to Choose a Score Goal

Your score goal is the score you hope to get on Test Day. It's the score you want to attain after studying in this course and preparing on your own. The key in choosing a score goal is to be realistic. Your score goal for each section should be about 40-50 points higher than what you scored on your first practice test. If you reach that goal on a later practice test, you can raise it.

Write your Diagnostic scores here:

Critical Reading: _____
Writing: _____

When you think about adding points to your score, consider your strengths and weaknesses.

Write your score goals here:

Critical Reading: _____
Writing: _____

Elements of Choosing a Score Goal

There are two main elements that factor into choosing a score goal:

How Many Questions to Answer

You do not need to answer every question to reach your score goal. For example, if your goal is to earn a 600 on Critical Reading, you need a raw score of around 50. That means you can skip 17 questions and achieve your score goal!

Which Questions to Answer

All questions on the SAT are worth: _SamE 1 point_____

To maximize your points, answer: _the questions you know_____

In the next few pages, you'll learn where to find the easier questions in the Critical Reading and Writing sections so you can pick up points quickly and efficiently.

Note: Photocopying any part of this book is prohibited by law.

34

Section Pacing: Critical Reading

The Critical Reading section is divided into two parts: Sentence Completion questions and Passage-based questions (Reading Comprehension).

Sentence Completions are arranged in order of difficulty. That means:

fill in the blanks, answer every easy question

Passage-based questions are not arranged in order of difficulty. That means:

answer the ones you know. Skim through the question

In choosing which questions to answer, consider the amount of time it takes to answer a question. Some questions that can be answered more quickly include:

Questions that take longer to answer include:

Section Pacing: Writing

The Writing portions of the test contain two types of questions: multiple-choice questions about writing and an essay that you write yourself.

The multiple-choice questions are arranged in order of difficulty. That means:

_____

_____

The essay is a little different, since it's just one question. That means:

_____

_____

How the Writing Section is Scored

- You get separate scores for the two question types.
- The multiple-choice questions are scored like the other questions on the test.
- The essay is scored on a scale of 0-6.
- Your two scores are combined to give you one overall writing score.

Note: Photocopying any part of this book is prohibited by law.

36

How Many Questions to Answer

Critical Reading

This table tells you how many questions you need to answer correctly for a variety of scores. Based on your score goals, figure out how many questions to answer.

Score Goal	Raw Points Needed	Questions to Answer
350	11	15
400	18	23
450	26	32
500	34	41
550	42	50
600	50	59
650	58	67

Questions to answer to meet your score goal for Critical Reading: _____

Writing

Figuring out how many multiple-choice questions to answer depends on how well you write. Sample scaled scores for different multiple-choice and essay raw scores:

MC Raw Score	Essay Score						
	0	1	2	3	4	5	6
45	570-690	580-720	600-740	630-770	670-800	700-800	730-800
40	520-640	530-670	550-690	580-710	620-750	650-780	680-800
35	480-590	490-620	510-640	540-670	570-710	610-740	640-770
30	430-550	450-580	470-600	500-630	530-660	560-700	590-720
25	390-510	410-540	430-560	450-580	490-620	520-650	550-680
20	360-470	370-500	390-520	420-550	460-580	490-620	520-640
15	310-430	330-460	350-480	380-510	410-540	440-570	470-600

Questions to answer to meet your score goal for Writing: _____

How to Tell if You Should Move On

On the SAT, questions fall into one of three categories.

- Questions You Know: You simply answer them and move on.

- Questions You Don't Know: If you have no idea how to approach a question, what the answer choices mean, or how to guess, skip it and move on. If you guess, chances are it will be wrong and will lose you points.

- Questions You Aren't Sure About: These are the tricky questions. Here's how to deal with them:

The Two-Pass Method

The First Pass
Start with early Sentence Completions, early Writing questions, and short passages. Answer as many as you can, then try to eliminate choices on questions that you might be able to answer. If you can eliminate two or three choices, guess aggressively from what's left and move on.

Next, try the long passages, focusing on the easier questions first, such as Detail questions and Vocabulary-in-Context. Leave the tricky Inference questions in particular for later.

Note in the test booklet any question you skip so that you can go back to it later. Also, when you skip a question, be careful to fill your next answer in the proper place on the answer sheet.

The Second Pass
Stop your first pass when you get to the harder questions in Sentence Completions and Writing, when you've gone through all the short passages, and you've given your best attempt at the long passage questions. Then go back to the questions you skipped and try them again.

If you make it through those questions and still have time left, see if any of the harder questions are in your areas of strength. However, do this only if you've spent enough time on the easy questions to be sure you got them right!

Note: Photocopying any part of this book is prohibited by law.

38

Summary

In this unit, you learned that:

- you can raise your score on Critical Reading and Writing by answering fewer questions.

- to maximize your score, answer earlier Sentence Completions and Writing questions, and those Reading Comprehension questions that you're likely to get right.

- you should use all of your time on the Essay, and make sure to leave two minutes at the end of the section to proofread your work.

- you can use the score goal tables to figure out roughly how many questions you need to answer to meet your Critical Reading and Writing score goals.

Session 2: Critical Reading Question Types

In this unit, you will learn to:

- recognize the three different types of Critical Reading questions.

- identify where Critical Reading questions appear on the test.

- draw connections between the skills Critical Reading questions test.

- expand your vocabulary efficiently to improve your performance on the Critical Reading sections.

The Critical Reading Sections

The Sections

The Critical Reading sections of the SAT are divided into three areas:

- Sentence Completions

_____

- Long Passages

_____

- Short Passages

_____

The Questions

Within these areas, you will see the following question types:

- Sentence Completions (the only type in this area)

- Main Idea questions

- Detail questions

- Vocabulary-in-Context questions

- Inference questions

- Compare and contrast questions

How do you feel about Critical Reading versus other sections of the SAT?

_____

_____

Sentence Completions

Each Sentence Completion question contains a sentence with a missing word or words. There will be one or two blanks, never more. Your job is to find the word or words that best fill in the blank or blanks.

Here is what a typical Sentence Completion question looks like:

1. After having spent the previous month relaxing at a cabin in the wilderness, Antonia found it ------- to readjust to city living.

(A) entertaining
(B) perplexing
(C) irrelevant
(D) challenging
(E) understandable

What makes this question type challenging?

_____

_____

What makes this question type manageable?

_____

_____

Long Passages

Where the Passages Appear

The Critical Reading sections on the SAT include four long passages with a total of about 40 questions.

- One section contains one long passage.

- Another section contains two long passages.

- Another section contains two related (paired) passages.

The majority of Critical Reading is long passages. What that means for you:

_____

_____

Passage Topics

The passages fall into three general subject areas:

- Natural sciences

- Social sciences

- Humanities

Long Passage Example

You don't need to read this whole passage now; just take a minute to familiarize yourself with the format. Notice that:

- The instructions appear above the passage. They are always the same.

- The italicized part in the beginning is the introductory material.

- Every fifth line is numbered.

The passage below is followed by questions based on its content. Answer the questions on the basis of what is stated or implied in the passage and in any introductory material that may be provided.

The following passage discusses the origins of the telegraph.

On the evening of April 18, 1775, Paul Revere set out on horseback to deliver an urgent message to the town of Lexington, Massachusetts: the British army was advancing by sea, signaling the beginning of the Revolutionary War. There was no Internet in 1775. For that matter, there were no telephones, no radios, no pagers, no
5 fax machines, and not even the grandfather of all these devices, the telegraph. Seventy years later, the message "The Redcoats Are Coming!" would have been sent out in dots and dashes over a telegraph wire, and Revere's famous ride would never have happened. However, with no other recourse, Revere hopped on his trusty horse and into the pages of history. Fifteen years later, a chain of scientific events
10 commenced that would culminate in an electronic communications revolution that would change the very nature of human interaction.

American painter and inventor Samuel Morse is the best-known name in the field of telegraphy, but as with most inventions, the story of the telegraph predates the contributions of its most visible progenitor. In the 1790s, Italian scientist Alessandro
15 Volta invented an electrochemical cell that produced a steady source of electric current. In 1820, Danish physicist Hans Christian Oersted discovered that an electric current can be used to cause a magnetized needle to move. Then in 1825, British inventor William Sturgeon (1783-1850) invented the electromagnet, the device that would eventually lay the foundations for large-scale electronic
20 communications. Sturgeon wrapped a seven-ounce piece of iron with wire, ran the current of a single-cell battery through it, and demonstrated that the device could lift nine pounds…

Long Passage Questions

Here are the nuts and bolts of the questions that follow long passages:

Each long passage is followed by 5-13 questions.

The questions are not arranged in order of difficulty. Rather, they follow the order of material presented in the passage.

The Questions

The questions after each passage include:

Main Idea:

_____

Detail:

_____

Vocabulary-in-Context:

_____

Inference:

_____

Compare and Contrast:

_____

Short Passages

Where Short Passages Appear

The Critical Reading sections on the SAT include about four short passages with a total of approximately eight questions. The questions are similar to those you'll see in the Long Passages portion.

- In one section, you'll see a set of Paired Short Passages.

- In another section, you'll see two unrelated Short Passages.

What Does a Short Passage Look Like?

Short passages consist of just one paragraph, and you can often get the gist of the main idea by reading the first and last sentences and skimming the middle. Here's an example of a short passage.

While some contend that a meteorite caused the cataclysmic mass extinction at the end of the Permian period, further studies do not bear this out. A more plausible theory concerns huge volcanic eruptions in Siberia that occurred at the same time as the extinctions. Researchers speculate that carbon dioxide released in the blasts increased the greenhouse effect, causing an increase in global temperatures that destabilized methane hydrate, a highly concentrated frozen gas. This methane release, scientists contend, further enhanced the greenhouse effect, resulting in runaway global warming that contributed to the extinction.

Note: Photocopying any part of this book is prohibited by law.

47

Comparing Short and Long Passages

What's the Same?

- You'll see the same question types.

- Easy questions are worth the same number of points as hard questions.

- If you can eliminate one or more answer choices, you should guess.

What this means for you: _____

_____

What's Different?

- Short Passages are just one paragraph, so you can easily skim a Short Passage before reading its questions.

- Short Passages are more direct than Long Passages.

What this means for you: _____

_____

SAT Vocabulary

There is no section on the SAT called "Vocabulary." So why is vocabulary important for succeeding on the test?

Sentence Completions:

_____

_____

Reading Comprehension:

_____

_____

Vocabulary-in-Context:

_____

_____

Should Vocabulary Be a Priority for You?

_____

_____

Learning Vocabulary

Your Turn

Which of the following approaches do you think will help you build your vocabulary for the SAT? Place a check mark next to each strategy you think would be helpful.

1. _____ Memorize the dictionary.

2. _____ Read more newspapers and books.

3. _____ Learn words in groups of similar meaning.

4. _____ Write down as many words as you can.

5. _____ Learn word roots and prefixes.

6. _____ Watch more TV.

7. _____ Analyze how context suggests word meanings.

Summary

In this unit, you learned that:

- Sentence Completion questions require you to fill in one or two blanks.

- Long Passages cover a variety of subjects.

- Long Passage questions appear in the order that information is presented in the passage.

- Short Passages consist of a brief paragraph.

- Short Passage questions are similar to Long Passage questions.

- having a strong vocabulary will help you succeed on the Critical Reading sections, but improving your reading skills should be your top priority.

Session 3: Math Strategy

In this unit, you will learn to:

- guess on the math questions with more confidence.

- make educated guesses by eliminating three common wrong answers.

- work backwards from the answer choices to help you answer questions correctly.

- plug in numbers to answer questions correctly.

- plug in numbers to answer questions involving percents.

- plug in numbers to answer questions involving remainders and hard fractions.

Guessing

If you can eliminate at least one choice, you can raise your score by guessing.

What should you do with questions that you can't solve?

Random Guessing

When you guess randomly, you choose answers without first eliminating choices.

On SAT multiple-choice questions, each wrong answer has a penalty of one quarter of a point.

If you choose randomly on 10 questions, odds are you'll:

get _2_ right and _8_ wrong.

gain _2_ points for your correct answers.

lose _2_ points for your wrong answers.

How many points do you gain by making random guesses? _____0_____

Educated Guessing

Educated guessing is guessing after eliminating one or more answer choices. This strategy earns you more points than you lose.

If you narrow each of 10 questions to 2 choices and guess on them, odds are you'll:

get _5_ right and _5_ wrong.

gain _5_ points for your correct answers.

lose _1/4_ points for your wrong answers.

How many points do you gain by making educated guesses? _3 3/4_

Is it worth it to guess if you can only narrow each question down to 3 or 4 choices?

Answers to Eliminate

What are the best ways to eliminate choices on questions you can't solve?

Wrong answers on the SAT fall into predictable categories. Here are three kinds of wrong answers that you should look to eliminate:

- Clunkers
- Obvious answers
- Rule breakers

Let's talk about each of these, and work through some examples.

Clunkers

Clunkers are answer choices that are simply not realistic.

When you read through the choices, you can usually recognize a clunker right away because it's just not possible given the numbers in the question.

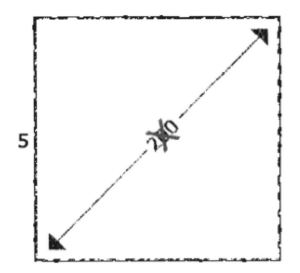

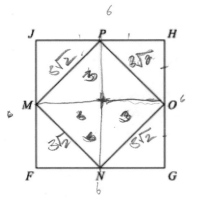

1. In the figure above, square *MNOP* is inscribed in square *FGHJ*. If the perimeter of *FGHJ* is 24 and *GO* = *OH*, what is the perimeter of square *MNOP*?

(A) $6\sqrt{2}$
(B) $8\sqrt{2}$
(C) $12\sqrt{2}$
(D) $18\sqrt{2}$
(E) $24\sqrt{2}$

Note: Photocopying any part of this book is prohibited by law.

57

Obvious Answers

Obvious answers are answer choices that result from overly simple calculations based on the numbers in the question.

2. A grocery store raised the price of a gallon of milk by 50%. During a sale the following week, however, the new price was reduced by 20%. After these two changes, by what percent had the price increased over the original price?

(A) 15%
(B) 20%
(C) 30%
(D) 40%
(E) 70%

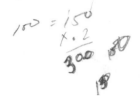

Rule Breakers

Rule breakers are answer choices that don't comply with standard rules of math or the information given in a particular question.

3. If m and n are positive integers and $5m + 2n = 9$, what is the value of $m + n$?

(A) 0
(B) 1
(C) 2
(D) 3
(E) 4

Note: Photocopying any part of this book is prohibited by law.

58

Elimination Practice Examples

Eliminate clunkers, obvious answers, and rule breakers in the following questions.

4. What is the least positive integer that is divisible by 5, 8, and 12?

(A) 60
(B) 90
(C) 120
(D) 240
(E) 480

5. Over the past year, the average price of a private home increased by 15%. If the average price was $200,000 a year ago, what is the average price now?

(A) $170,000
(B) $203,000
(C) $215,000
(D) $230,000
(E) $300,000

6. In order to prepare for a raffle, Miles wrote the numbers 1 through 30 on individual slips of paper and placed them in a large bowl. In doing so, how many digits did he write?

(A) 30
(B) 50
(C) 51
(D) 59
(E) 60

Note: Photocopying any part of this book is prohibited by law.

59

Working Backwards

Yadda yadda yadda, yadda yadda yadda yadda?

(A) 2
(B) 3
(C) 4
(D) 5
(E) 6

When to Work Backwards

Work backwards when:

- you are asked to solve an equation.
- you have a word problem.
- the answer choices are numbers.

Some questions probably won't be good for working backwards:

- questions with variables in the answer choices

- questions that don't ask a direct question (for example, "Which of the following is NOT...?")

Note: Photocopying any part of this book is prohibited by law.

60

Working Backwards Method

There are three steps involved in working backwards. Let's go through them one at a time.

Step 1

Start with the middle choice.

7. In a spice shop, cayenne pepper is sold for 50 cents per ounce for the first ounce, and 35 cents per ounce for any ounce after the first ounce. How many ounces of cayenne pepper can be bought for $2.95?

(A) 7
(B) 8
(C) 9
(D) 10
(E) 11

Step 2

Eliminate choices that are too big or too small.
If choice (C) is too small, then everything less than (C) must also be too small. If choice (C) is too big, then everything greater than (C) must also be too big.

7. In a spice shop, cayenne pepper is sold for 50 cents per ounce for the first ounce, and 35 cents per ounce for any ounce after the first ounce. How many ounces of cayenne pepper can be bought for $2.95?

(A) 7
(B) 8
(C) 9
(D) 10
(E) 11

Step 3

Test one of the remaining choices.

You only need to try one more choice. If it works, pick it. If it doesn't work, the other choice must be correct, so pick that one. Try the choice that makes the math easiest to do.

7. In a spice shop, cayenne pepper is sold for 50 cents per ounce for the first ounce, and 35 cents per ounce for any ounce after the first ounce. How many ounces of cayenne pepper can be bought for $2.95?

(A) 7
(B) 8
(C) 9
(D) 10
(E) 11

Working Backwards Practice Questions

Work backwards to answer these practice questions.

8. If $\dfrac{x}{4} = \dfrac{3}{8}$, then $x =$ *(handwritten: $8x = \frac{12}{8} = x = \frac{3}{2}$)*

(A) $\dfrac{4}{3}$

(B) $\dfrac{3}{2}$ *(circled)*

(C) 2

(D) 6

(E) 12

9. If $2x - 5 = 7$, then $x =$ *(handwritten: $\frac{2x}{2} = \frac{12}{2}$ $x = 6$)*

(A) 3

(B) 4

(C) 5

(D) 6 *(circled)*

(E) 7

10. Stephen can pick 2 pails of cherries in 1 hour. Joe can pick 3 pails of cherries in 2 hours. How long would it take Stephen and Joe to pick 14 pails of cherries if they worked together at their individual rates?

(A) 2 hours

(B) 3 hours

(C) 4 hours *(circled)*

(D) 5 hours

(E) 6 hours

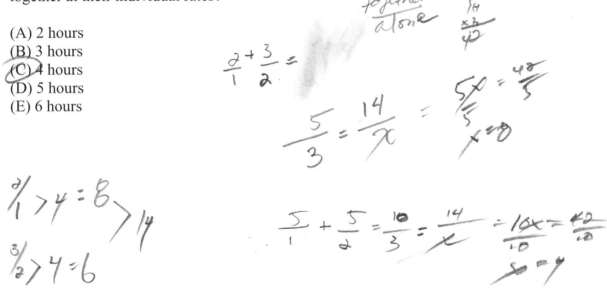

Plugging in Numbers (PIN)

When to PIN

You should plug in numbers when:

- the answer choices contain variables (such as *x, y, k,* or some other letter standing in for a number).

- the question involves percents, fractions, or ratios, but no actual numbers are given.

When Not to PIN

You should not plug in numbers when the answer choices contain numbers (not variables, percents, or ratios).

PIN Method

Step 1

Pick a simple number to replace the variable.

Tip: Always pick a number that's easy to work with, like 2 or 3. Small integers are usually best. Remember to jot down the number you pick so you don't forget it.

11. What is the end result if 4 is added to x and this sum is divided by 2?

(A) $4 + \dfrac{x}{2}$

(B) $2 + \dfrac{x}{2}$

(C) $2 + x$

(D) $4 + x$

(E) $\dfrac{x}{2}$

Step 2

Plug that number into the question stem.

Replace *x* with 2, and do the math using that number.

11. What is the end result if 4 is added to *x* and this sum is divided by 2?

(A) $4 + \dfrac{x}{2}$

(B) $2 + \dfrac{x}{2}$

(C) $2 + x$

(D) $4 + x$

(E) $\dfrac{x}{2}$

Our target number is  _____.

Step 3

Plug the number into the answer choices. Eliminate those that give a different result from the target number.

11. What is the end result if 4 is added to *x* and this sum is divided by 2?

(A) $4 + \dfrac{x}{2}$

(B) $2 + \dfrac{x}{2}$

(C) $2 + x$

(D) $4 + x$

(E) $\dfrac{x}{2}$

PIN and Percents

Often, questions will talk about percents but will not refer to actual numbers.

12. If a number x is decreased by 10 percent and then this value is increased by 20 percent, what percent is the final value of the original value of x?

(A) 90%
(B) 108%
(C) 110%
(D) 130%
(E) 132%

Note: Photocopying any part of this book is prohibited by law.

66

Plugging In on Remainders

13. When *m* is divided by 8, the remainder is 3, and when *n* is divided by 8, the remainder is 6. What is the remainder when $m + n$ is divided by 8?

(A) 0
(B) 1
(C) 3
(D) 5
(E) 9

What are the most logical numbers to plug in here?

Plugging In on Questions with a Lot of Fractions

You can use plugging in on the following hard fraction problem since it never asks you for an actual number of surfboards, only fractions of some generic number of surfboards.

14. Two thirds of Marcus's surfboards are six feet long, and $\frac{3}{5}$ of the remaining surfboards are eight feet long. What fraction of Marcus's surfboards are neither six feet long nor eight feet long?

(A) $\frac{1}{15}$

(B) $\frac{2}{15}$

(C) $\frac{1}{5}$

(D) $\frac{4}{5}$

(E) $\frac{13}{5}$

What numbers should you plug in for this one?

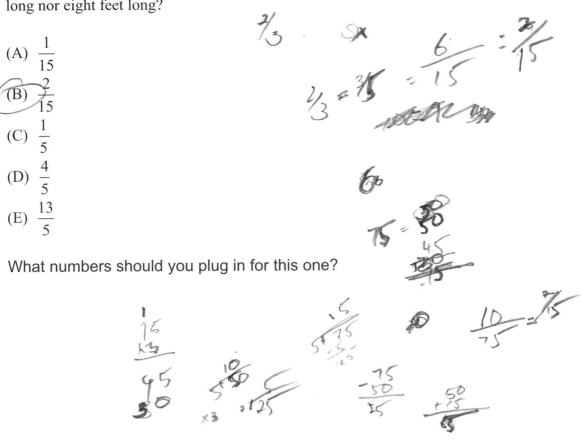

PIN Practice Questions

Plug in numbers to solve these questions.

15. If $x = 3y + 4$ then $3x - y =$

(A) $9y - 4$
(B) $9y - 12$
(C) $6y + 12$
(D) $6y + 8$
(E) $8y + 12$

16. If n is an odd integer, what is the next greatest odd integer in terms of n?

(A) $n + 1$
(B) $n + 2$
(C) $n + 3$
(D) $2n$
(E) $3n$

17. If the budget for a department is reduced by 25 percent, and then that amount is reduced by a further 25 percent, what percent of the original budget is the final budget?

(A) 42.5%
(B) 50%
(C) 56.25%
(D) 66%
(E) 75%

Summary

In this unit, you learned that:

- making educated guesses on the SAT will raise your score.

- you can eliminate Clunkers, Obvious Answers, and Rule Breakers.

- working backwards helps you answer word problems simply.

- plugging in numbers turns algebra into arithmetic.

- percents problems are much easier to solve when you plug in 100.

- you can use plugging in to help you solve problems with remainders and fractions.

Answer Key

1. C
2. B
3. D
4. C
5. D
6. C
7. B
8. B
9. D
10. C
11. B
12. B
13. B
14. B
15. E
16. B
17. C

Note: Photocopying any part of this book is prohibited by law.

70

Session 3: Writing Question Types

In this unit, you will learn:

- what the SAT Writing question types are.

- how to approach the different question types.

Writing Sections

The SAT includes three Writing sections: One is an essay section, and the other two are multiple choice.

You'll learn about the essay section later in this unit. Now, you'll learn about the three different types of questions that you'll see in the multiple-choice SAT Writing sections:

- Error Identification
- Sentence Improvement
- Paragraph Improvement

The following pages provide a general introduction to each type.

Error Identification Questions

An Error Identification question contains a single sentence with four underlined words or groups of words.

Your job is to evaluate the underlined portions and determine which one, if any, contains a mistake. If you find a mistake in portion A, for example, you fill in choice (A) on your answer sheet.

Here's an example of an Error Identification question:

1. The main <u>focus of the textbook</u> in the course, <u>which</u>
              A   B

   spans two centuries of literature, <u>are</u> the ways in which
                                 C

   human relationships <u>develop</u> and subsequently evolve. <u>No error</u>
                       D   E

Solving Error Identification Questions

Solve Error Identification questions with Peterson's 3-Step Method:

1) **Read the sentence.** As you read, sort each underlined portion into categories: Definitely Correct, Definitely Incorrect, and Not Sure.

2) **Pick your answer.** Optimally, you'll find only one Definitely Incorrect portion; if not, move on to step 3.

3) **Reread the sentence.** If you're not sure of the correct answer, or if you think there are no errors, take another look, checking for classic SAT writing errors (you'll learn about these shortly).

Now try solving this Error Identification question using the 3-Step Method.

1. The main <u>focus of the textbook</u> in the course, <u>which</u>
                    A   B

spans two centuries of literature, <u>are</u> the ways in which
                                     C

human relationships <u>develop </u>and subsequently evolve. <u>No error</u>
                      D   E

Do any choices leap out as being Definitely Incorrect? How about Definitely Correct?

Sentence Improvement Questions

Each question is a sentence with an underlined portion. The underlined portion may contain a mistake, but it doesn't always. Choice (A) is the original underlined portion, exactly as written. The other four choices contain different versions of the underlined portion.

Your job is to determine whether one of the answer choices is better than the original underlined portion. If you think the original version is best, pick choice (A). If not, select the choice that you feel best substitutes for the underlined potion of the sentence.

Here's an example of a Sentence Improvement question:

2. Scientists have recently discovered enzymes that can be used both to speed <u>oxidation and forming new proteins</u>.

(A) oxidation and forming new proteins
(B) oxidation and formed new proteins
(C) oxidation, as well as, forming new proteins
(D) oxidation and to form new proteins
(E) the oxidation and forming new proteins

Solving Sentence Improvement Questions

Follow Peterson's Technique for Sentence Improvement questions:

1) **Read the entire sentence.** As you do, try to determine the construction employed in the underlined portion. For example, does it contain a verb phrase? A description?

2) **Determine whether the underlined portion contains a mistake.** Even if you're pretty sure the original version is correct, it's a good idea to skim the choices to make sure.

3) **Evaluate the choices.** Don't waste time reading choice (A)—it's always the same as the underlined portion. You don't always need to read each choice in its entirety. Instead, look for the differences among the choices. That'll point you to where the mistake is.

Now try to solve this Sentence Improvement question.

2. Scientists have recently discovered enzymes that can be used both to speed <u>oxidation and forming new proteins</u>.

(A) oxidation and forming new proteins
(B) oxidation and formed new proteins
(C) oxidation, as well as, forming new proteins
(D) oxidation and to form new proteins
(E) the oxidation and forming new proteins

What does the underlined portion do?

_____

Which parts of the answer choices are all the same?

_____

Which parts are different?

_____

Note: Photocopying any part of this book is prohibited by law.

76

Paragraph Improvement Questions

Paragraph Improvement questions consist of a short passage, usually two to four paragraphs in length. The passage represents a draft of an essay, and each sentence of the passage is numbered. Your job is to read the passage and answer questions about how to improve it.

The questions usually will not focus on grammar. Instead, they will ask how ideas or connections in the passage might be made clearer.

These questions generally take more time than the other question types, so you may wish to tackle them after you've finished the other questions in the section.

You're likely to see three types of Paragraph Improvement questions:

- Author's purpose: these ask about why an author made a particular writing choice.

- Style: these ask you to evaluate language choices, sentence flow, and other stylistic elements.

- Organization: these ask how material is organized in a passage; for example, introductions, transitions, conclusions, and so on.

Here's an example of a Paragraph Improvement question:

(1) New archaeological digs and techniques are changing our view of the distant past. (2) Anatolia was once thought to be the earliest known agricultural-based city. (3) Recent evidence, however, indicates that in Anatolia hunting and gathering continued to be key to survival long after that dense settlement was built.

3. In context, which is the most logical word or phrase to insert at the beginning of sentence 2?

(A) For example,
(B) Predictably,
(C) Moreover,
(D) Furthermore,
(E) But anyway,

Solving Paragraph Improvement Questions

To solve Paragraph Improvement questions, consider the context of the word, phrase, sentence, or paragraph in question. That means you have to read the material that surrounds it.

Try answering this Paragraph Improvement question:

(1) New archaeological digs and techniques are changing our view of the distant past. (2) Anatolia was once thought to be the earliest known agricultural-based city. (3) Recent evidence, however, indicates that in Anatolia hunting and gathering continued to be key to survival long after that dense settlement was built.

3. In context, which is the most logical word or phrase to insert at the beginning of sentence 2?

(A) For example,
(B) Predictably,
(C) Moreover,
(D) Furthermore,
(E) But anyway,

What type of Paragraph Improvement question is this?

_____

What clues in the passage help you answer the question?

_____

Paragraph Improvement Practice Questions

(1) Watching a film adaptation of a novel is a very different experience from reading the book. (2) When a novel is made into a film, for example, certain things are different. (3) If you read the novel before you watch the film adaptation, you might find yourself wondering what happened to your favorite minor characters and most of the story. (4) The answer is that they were deemed less important than keeping a movie down to a two-hour running time.

4. The author could make sentence 2 provide a specific example by changing certain things are different to

(A) a great deal might have changed
(B) many of the characters and much of the story are cut
(C) differences, and some of them significant, are likely to appear
(D) there are definite differences between the novel and the film
(E) some people will prefer to watch a movie rather than read a book

What type of Paragraph Improvement question is this?

_____

What clues in the passage help you answer the question?

_____

(1) A major goal of the Viking spacecraft missions of the late 1980s was to determine whether the soil of Mars is dead, like the soil of the moon. (2) Or teeming with microscopic life, like the soils of Earth. (3) (4) Soil samples brought into the Viking lander were sent to three separate biological laboratories to be tested in different ways for the presence of living things.

5. Which is the best way to write the underlined portion of sentences 1 and 2, reproduced below?

A major goal of the Viking spacecraft missions of the late 1980s was to determine whether the soil of Mars is dead, like the soil of the <u>moon. Or teeming with</u> microscopic life, like the soils of Earth.

(A) moon. Or teeming with
(B) moon or is it teeming with
(C) moon, or teeming with
(D) moon. Or, on the other hand, is it teeming with
(E) moon or teeming. With

Essay Section

The essay section of the SAT gives you a topic to write about, called a prompt. The prompt will ask you to consider a particular issue or idea, and write an essay presenting your opinion about it.

Your job is to:

- develop a point of view.
- support your point of view with reasoning, evidence, and observations.
- demonstrate a command of standard written English.

There is no right or wrong answer to an essay topic. What's important is not which side you pick—it's how well you express yourself.

Here's a sample prompt:

> Directions: Think carefully about the issue presented in the following quote and the assignment below.
>
> "First I saw the mountains in the painting; then I saw the painting in the mountains."
>
> -- Chinese Proverb
>
> **Assignment:** What is your view on the idea that art, rather than being a reflection of the world, can help us see the real world in new ways? Plan and write an essay in which you develop your point of view on this issue. Support your position with reasoning and examples taken from your reading, studies, experience, or observations.

Later units will be devoted to strategies for crafting a polished and coherent essay.

Summary

In this unit, you learned that:

- Error Identification questions ask you to choose which part of a sentence, if any, contains an error.

- Sentence Improvement questions ask you to choose the correct version of an underlined portion of a sentence.

- Paragraph Improvement questions ask you to analyze an essay draft and to consider the context in which the writing elements in question appear.

- Essay questions ask you to respond to a prompt.

Answer Key

1. C
2. D
3. A
4. B
5. C

Session 3: Reading the Passage

In this unit, you will learn to:

- use Peterson's 4-Step Method to approach Critical Reading passages.

- recognize the major types of Critical Reading passage-based questions.

- decide which question types to focus on first.

Peterson's 4-Step Method for Critical Reading Passages

A long Critical Reading passage and a bunch of questions might seem intimidating. Don't worry—use Peterson's 4-Step Method to approach them.

1. Read the introduction.

2. Read the first half of the passage.

3. Answer as many questions as you can.

4. Use the remaining questions to guide your reading of the rest of the passage.

Let's talk about what kinds of questions you're likely to see so you can decide which to tackle first. You'll apply the method to a passage shortly.

Note: Photocopying any part of this book is prohibited by law.

84

Deciding Which Questions to Solve

You probably won't solve all of the questions in a set. Which should you solve, and which are more trouble than they're worth?

These are the different passage-based question types you can expect to see. As you look at each one, think about whether it looks like a question you should solve right away or one that should wait until after you've solved the easier ones.

Main Idea Questions

The main purpose of this passage is to

(A) list the different styles of American music
(B) show that jazz is the only true form of American music
(C) argue that rural music had a large influence on urban music
(D) explain the evolution of American musical styles
(E) encourage the reader to listen to more American music

How should you prioritize this question type?

Detail Questions

The third paragraph describes the author as

(A) an avid historian
(B) an accomplished musician
(C) a person with few opinions
(D) a lover of all music
(E) an expert on American culture

How should you prioritize this question type?

Vocabulary-in-Context Questions

In line 34, "short" most closely means

(A) lacking
(B) behind
(C) brief
(D) impossible
(E) broke

How should you prioritize this question type?

Inference Questions

The author implies that a "true musical tradition" (line 74) must include

(A) a completely unique sound
(B) a blend of cultural influences
(C) a variety of instruments
(D) improvisation
(E) room for change

How should you prioritize this question type?

"Why?" Questions

The author uses the phrase "breadth of vision" in order to

(A) suggest that early American musicians lacked foresight
(B) imply that modern American music has failed to uphold the standards of its predecessors
(C) show the extent to which music has changed over the years
(D) illustrate the creative process of musicians
(E) argue that music is the most illuminating of all art forms

How should you prioritize this question type?

Step 1: Reading the Introduction

Now that you've learned how to prioritize the question types, let's go back to the 4-Step Method.

Step 1 is reading the introduction, which is the italicized part at the beginning of the passage. Here's an example:

> *The following passage discusses the origins of the telegraph.*

What information does this introduction give you?

Step 2: Reading the First Half of the Passage

After you read the introduction, read the first half of the passage, which will be roughly two paragraphs long. It will give you a good understanding of the main idea and overall tone of the passage.

The following passage discusses the origins of the telegraph.

On the evening of April 18, 1775, Paul Revere set out on horseback to deliver an urgent message to the town of Lexington, Massachusetts: the British army was advancing by sea, signaling the beginning of the Revolutionary War. There was no Internet in 1775. For that matter, there were no telephones, no radios, no pagers, no
5   fax machines, and not even the grandfather of all these devices, the telegraph. Seventy years later, the message "The Redcoats Are Coming!" would have been sent out in dots and dashes over a telegraph wire, and Revere's famous ride would never have happened. However, with no other recourse, Revere hopped on his trusty horse and into the pages of history. Fifteen years later, a chain of scientific events
10 commenced that would culminate in an electronic communications revolution that would change the very nature of human interaction.

American painter and inventor Samuel Morse is the best-known name in the field of telegraphy, but as with most inventions, the story of the telegraph predates the contributions of its most visible progenitor. In the 1790s, Italian scientist Alessandro
15 Volta invented an electrochemical cell that produced a steady source of electric current. In 1820, Danish physicist Hans Christian Oersted discovered that an electric current can be used to cause a magnetized needle to move. Then in 1825, British inventor William Sturgeon (1783-1850) invented the electromagnet, the device that would eventually lay the foundations for large-scale electronic
20 communications. Sturgeon wrapped a seven-ounce piece of iron with wire, ran the current of a single-cell battery through it, and demonstrated that the device could lift nine pounds.

Based on the first half of the passage, what do you know about the passage's tone and subject matter?

Step 3: Answering Questions from the First Half of the Passage

Skim the questions below and think about which ones to answer at this stage.

1. The phrase "grandfather of all these devices" (line 5) suggests that

(A) the telegraph descends directly from telephones, radios, pagers, and fax machines
(B) if Paul Revere had access to a telegraph in 1775, the war would not have happened
(C) the telegraph is the most efficient way to communicate during a war
(D) the telegraph spawned later forms of communication technology
(E) Paul Revere's relatives fought in the Revolutionary War

2. According to the passage, Paul Revere delivered his message by horseback because

(A) in 1775 a message delivered by horseback arrived faster than by telegraph
(B) that was the only viable means available at the time
(C) the telephones and radios in Lexington were not working properly
(D) of the high probability that the British would intercept a telegraph transmission
(E) he knew the drama of his ride would make him famous

3. The author relates the story of Paul Revere in the first paragraph primarily in order to

(A) argue that history cannot be separated from technological advances
(B) illustrate the evolution of the telegraph
(C) underscore the importance of communication in military matters
(D) compare the impact of messages delivered by various forms of communication technologies
(E) supply a historical context for the invention of the telegraph

4. In line 14, "its most visible progenitor" refers to

(A) the telegraph
(B) the power source of the telegraph
(C) Samuel Morse
(D) Alessandro Volta
(E) most inventions

5. Joseph Henry's scientific contribution

(A) relied upon the discoveries of Volta, Oersted, and Sturgeon
(B) was seen by most as the herald of new age of electronic communication
(C) initiated the chain of events that culminated in the invention of the telegraph
(D) was the invention of the telegraph
(E) was the result of a collaborative effort between Cooke, Wheatstone, and Henry

Step 4: Tackling the Rest of the Questions

Here is the rest of the passage.

Building on this achievement, American Joseph Henry (1797-1878) demonstrated in 1830 the potential of Sturgeon's device for long distance communication by
25 sending an electronic current over one mile of wire to activate an electromagnet which caused a bell to strike. Morse combined the fact that an electric current can cause a distant bell to ring with the idea that the current can be varied systematically according to a code, and gave birth to modern telegraphy. Most who heard about Henry's experiment imagined a simple bell ringing. Samuel Morse heard the death
30 knell of the pony express and the thundering herald of a new age of electronic communication. British physicists William F. Cooke and Charles Wheatstone also parlayed these previous discoveries into the invention of the telegraph. The Morse telegraph—introduced in 1837 but not fully functional until 1844—was most successful for a number of reasons, including its simple operation and its relatively
35 low cost. Morse used pulses of current to deflect a remote electromagnet, which moved a marker to emboss paper with dots and dashes using the now universalized Morse Code. The telegraph changes the dots and dashes of this code into electrical impulses and transmits them over telegraph wires, later to reappear as dots and dashes on paper at the message destination.
40 Besides being the forerunner of all electronic communication, the telegraph represented the first application of paper tapes as a medium for the preparation, storage, and transmission of data, a technique that would eventually be used by the designers of the computer. This method was also used for the transmission and recording of stock market quotes. The massive volumes of paper used in this
45 endeavor spawned the cultural phenomenon of the "ticker-tape parade," whereby thousands of tons of old ticker tape were shredded and showered over visiting luminaries in New York City's Canyon of Heroes. Such a parade honoring Samuel Morse would have been both ironic and fitting.

Step 4 is to use the remaining questions to guide your reading of the rest of the passage. How might you work through the rest of the questions presented below?

6. The author's description of Morse's reaction to Henry's experiment (lines 26-31) is most likely intended to

(A) discredit the claim that Henry should be considered the true inventor of the telegraph
(B) prove that Morse was smarter than others who heard about Henry's experiment
(C) demonstrate Morse's belief that Henry's experiment had far-reaching implications
(D) explain why Morse's telegraph was more successful than the Cooke and Wheatstone telegraph
(E) shed light on Morse's disdain for the pony express

7. The passage indicates which of the following as a reason for the success of Morse's telegraph?

(A) bold marketing
(B) American ingenuity
(C) the use of electrical impulses to produce dots and dashes
(D) ease of use
(E) advanced workmanship

8. The description of the "ticker-tape parade" (line 45) illustrates

(A) the flexibility with which the Morse telegraph operated
(B) the appreciation the public had for Morse's invention
(C) an ironclad relationship between technology and culture
(D) a clever use of culture to overcome one of the major problems of the telegraph
(E) how unintended uses may emerge from technological advancements

9. In line 48, "fitting" most nearly means

(A) jubilant
(B) attachment
(C) sizable
(D) appropriate
(E) sarcastic

Reading Short Passages

Some Critical Reading passages are far shorter than the full-length passages found throughout the test. When reading these short passages, keep the following tips in mind:

- Pay careful attention to the first sentence, which usually presents the main idea.

- Don't try to memorize the details in the middle of the paragraph—you can look them up later if you need them.

- Pay careful attention to the last sentence, which often sums up the main idea or draws a conclusion.

Short Passage Examples

While some contend that a meteorite caused the cataclysmic mass extinction at the end of the Permian period, further studies do not bear this out. A more plausible theory concerns huge volcanic eruptions in Siberia that occurred at the same time as the extinctions. Researchers speculate that carbon dioxide released in the blasts increased the greenhouse effect, causing an increase in global temperatures that destabilized methane hydrate, a highly concentrated frozen gas. This methane release, scientists contend, further enhanced the greenhouse effect, resulting in runaway global warming that contributed to the extinction.

10. As used in line 2, "bear this out" most nearly means

(A) endure this
(B) refute this
(C) assume this
(D) support this
(E) explain this

11. In the passage, the author is primarily interested in

(A) reassessing the cause of a natural phenomenon
(B) moderating a debate between the proponents of conflicting theories
(C) challenging the assumptions underlying a scientific hypothesis
(D) reinterpreting evidence in order to lend support to a course of action
(E) calling a theory into question by exposing the motives of its supporters

Note: Photocopying any part of this book is prohibited by law.

92

The Amish live according to principles that are often in sharp contrast to the values of American culture, but conflicts between the Amish and the government have been resolved through mutual compromise. Although initially reluctant to send their children to public school, the Amish finally conceded that allowing their children to experience the outside world would make them truly appreciate the meaning of being Amish. However, they opposed the law requiring attendance through high school. Ultimately, the U.S. Supreme Court ruled in their favor.

12. This passage is primarily about

(A) ways that the Amish are different from mainstream Americans
(B) the inability of people with different ideas to understand each other
(C) how much mainstream Americans would benefit from more interaction with the Amish
(D) the way two very different cultures have worked out their differences
(E) the history of the Amish people in America

13. The author states that the Amish were "initially reluctant to send their children to public school" (lines 3-4) primarily in order to

(A) demonstrate the government's position toward the Amish
(B) prove that the Amish oppose all forms of public education
(C) illustrate the core beliefs of the Amish people
(D) show that the Amish sought interaction with mainstream culture
(E) provide background to an example of the Amish's compromise with the government

Summary

In this unit, you learned that:

- you should always read the introduction to a passage.

- you should read the first half of the passage and then look to answer questions based on that material.

- you should let the remaining questions guide you through the rest of the passage, determining what you should read in-depth and what you should skim over.

- some questions are easier to answer than others.

- when reading short passages, read for the main idea and return to the details only when necessary.

Answer Key

1. D
2. B
3. E
4. C
5. A
6. C
7. D
8. E
9. D
10. D
11. A
12. D
13. E

Session 4: Number Properties

In this unit, you will:

- learn the definition of an integer.

- learn the properties of positive, negative, even, and odd numbers.

- work with consecutive numbers.

- work with prime numbers.

- learn about factors and multiples.

- learn to calculate greatest common factors and least common multiples.

Note: Photocopying any part of this book is prohibited by law.

95

Definition of an Integer

An integer is a number that's not a decimal or fraction. An integer can be positive, negative, or zero.

Can you think of 5 integers?

Can you think of five numbers that aren't integers?

1. Which of the following numbers is not an integer?

(A) –6
(B) 0
(C) $\dfrac{1}{2}$
(D) 19
(E) 275

2. If r is an integer, all of the following must be integers EXCEPT:

(A) $r - 2r$
(B) $r + 11$
(C) $\dfrac{r}{r}$
(D) $\dfrac{r}{2}$
(E) $\dfrac{-2r}{r}$

Positive and Negative Numbers

A positive number is any number greater than 0.

A negative number is any number less than 0.

0 is neither positive nor negative.

positive $\times$ positive =
positive $\times$ negative =
negative $\times$ negative =

positive $\div$ positive =
positive $\div$ negative =
negative $\div$ negative =

3. If x is positive and y is negative, which of the following could be the value of xy?

(A) -6
(B) 0
(C) 1
(D) 2.5
(E) 10

Note: Photocopying any part of this book is prohibited by law.

97

Even and Odd Numbers

An even number is an integer divisible by 2.

An odd number is an integer not divisible by 2.

even + even =
even + odd =

even − even =
even − odd =
odd − even =

even × even =
even × odd =
odd × odd =

4. If x is an integer, which of the following must be an odd integer?

(A) $x + 1$
(B) $2x$
(C) $2x - 1$
(D) x^2
(E) $x^2 + 1$

Note: Photocopying any part of this book is prohibited by law.

98

Consecutive Numbers

Consecutive numbers are evenly-spaced numbers that follow each other:

1, 2, 3, 4, 5, _____, _____, _____

−12, −11, −10, _____, _____, _____

−1, 0, 1, _____, _____, _____

Consecutive even integers follow one another successively, skipping by twos:

2, 4, 6, _____, _____, _____

−12, −10, _____, _____, _____

−4, −2, 0, _____, _____, _____

Consecutive odd integers also follow one another successively, skipping by twos, but they are all odd numbers:

1, 3, 5, _____, _____, _____

−11, −9, −7, _____, _____, _____

−3, −1, 1, 3, _____, _____, _____

The best way to approach consecutive integer questions is by working backwards or plugging in.

5. The sum of three consecutive odd integers is 21. What is the smallest of these integers?

(A) 5
(B) 6
(C) 7
(D) 17
(E) 19

If you see a Grid-in question involving consecutive numbers, you may be able to plug in.

6. If x, y, and z are consecutive even integers, what is the value of $z - x$?

Prime Numbers

A prime number is an integer greater than 1 that is only divisible by itself and 1.

- 1 is not a prime number.
- Negative numbers cannot be prime.
- Zero is not prime.

The first four prime numbers are 2, 3, _____, and ____

No even number, except for 2, is prime, because all even numbers (other than 2) are divisible by themselves, 1, and 2.

7. How many prime numbers are there between 20 and 40, inclusive?

Note: Photocopying any part of this book is prohibited by law.

101

Factors and Multiples

A factor of an integer is an integer that can be divided evenly into that number.

Factors of 6 are 1, 2, 3, and 6

What are the factors of 10?

What are the factors of 36?

A prime factor of a number is a factor of that number that is prime.

The prime factors of 6 are 2 and 3.

What are the prime factors of 36?

A multiple of an integer has that number as a factor.

Multiples of 6 are 6, 12, 18, 24, 30...

What are the first five multiples of 10?

What are the first five multiples of 36?

8. Which of the following numbers is a factor of 72 but is NOT a multiple of 3?

(A) 3
(B) 4
(C) 6
(D) 12
(E) 16

Greatest Common Factor

The greatest common factor (GCF) is the largest factor that two or more numbers have in common.

9. What is the greatest factor that 54 and 72 have in common?

(A) 4
(B) 6
(C) 12
(D) 18
(E) 24

Least Common Multiples

The least common multiple (LCM) is the smallest multiple that two or more numbers have in common.

To find the LCM, list the first few multiples of each number. Identify the smallest number they have in common.

10. What is the least common multiple of 24 and 32?

(A) 48
(B) 64
(C) 72
(D) 96
(E) 128

Summary

In this unit, you learned that:

- integers are numbers that are not decimals or fractions. They can be positive, negative, or zero.

- positive and negative numbers yield predictable results when multiplied or divided by one another.

- even and odd numbers yield predictable results when added to, subtracted from, or multiplied by one another.

- working backwards and plugging in are valuable strategies for solving consecutive integer problems.

- a prime number is an integer greater than 1 that is only divisible by itself and 1.

- the greatest common factor is the largest factor that two or more numbers have in common.

- the least common multiple is the smallest multiple that two or more numbers have in common.

Answer Key

1. C
2. D
3. A
4. C
5. A
6. 4
7. 4
8. B
9. D
10. D

Session 4: Word Problems

In this unit, you will learn to:

- understand and apply the secret to solving word problems.

- translate English into math.

- work through word problems of all different types.

- approach data interpretation problems.

Note: Photocopying any part of this book is prohibited by law.

105

The Secret of Word Problems

Read the Question

To raise your score, you need to make sure you read the question carefully before beginning your calculations, and again before entering your final answer.

Why should you read a word problem twice?

_____

1. George and Isabel volunteered to paint a community center. Combined, they worked a total of 100 hours. If George worked $\frac{2}{3}$ the number of hours that Isabel did, how many hours did George work?

2. If $x + y = 7$, and $y = 3$, then what is the value of $2x$?

Translation

English	Math	Example	Translation
What, a number	x, n, etc.	**A number** is equal to itself squared.	$x = x^2$
Equals, is, was, Has, costs	$=$	Tom **is** 18 years old. A pickle **costs** 5 cents.	$t = 18$ $p = 5$
More, more than, greater than, added to, total, sum, increased by	$+$	Tom has $3 **more than** Sally. Tom and Sally have a **total** of $5.	$t = s + 3$ $t + s = 5$
Less than, smaller than, decreased by, difference, fewer	$-$	Sally has three **fewer** dollars than Tom. The **difference** between Tom's and Sally's savings in $3.	$s = t - 3$ $t - s = 3$
Of, times, Product of, twice, double, triple, half of, quarter of	$\times$	Tom has **twice** as much money as Sally. Rob's savings is **triple** Tom's savings.	$t = 2 \times s$ $r = 3 \times t$
Divided by, per, for, out of, ratio of, ___ to ___	$\div$	Sally has $1 **for** every $2 Tom has. The **ratio of** Tom's savings to Sally's savings is 2 to 1.	$s = t \div 2$ $\dfrac{t}{s} = \dfrac{2}{1}$

Your Turn

Now fill in the math equivalents for these sentences.

English Sentence	Math Equation
Trent has three dollars less than Kate.	
Kate has two pencils for every pencil Tent has.	
Trent has twice as many rabbits as Kate has.	
The ratio of Trent's score to Kate's score is 1:4.	
The sum of Trent and Kate's income is $100 less than twice Kate's income.	

Common Translation Errors

How would you translate the statement below into a mathematical expression?

Joe has 5 fewer dollars than Ali.

Another major error in translation is failing to convert percents, decimals, and fractions correctly.

Algebra Word Problems

3. Tina has x more dollars than Alan has, and together they have a total of y dollars. Which of the following represents the number of dollars that Alan has?

(A) $y - 2x$
(B) $2y - x$
(C) $\dfrac{y}{2} - x$
(D) $y - \dfrac{x}{2}$
(E) $\dfrac{y - x}{2}$

Algebra Word Problem Strategies

You can use translation, PIN, or working backwards to answer algebra word problems.

4. Kenny had twice as many comic books as Gil had. After giving Gil 7 comic books, Kenny has 6 more comic books than Gil has. How many comic books did Kenny have originally?

(A) 26
(B) 30
(C) 36
(D) 40
(E) 44

5. In a group of 78 children, there are 24 more girls than boys. How many girls are in the group?

(A) 37
(B) 48
(C) 51
(D) 54
(E) 57

Note: Photocopying any part of this book is prohibited by law.

109

Data Interpretation

You can expect to see about three Data Interpretation questions on your SAT. They can appear in either the Problem Solving or Grid-In question sets.

Peterson's Three-Step Method

Step 1: Read the question carefully.

Step 2: Examine the chart or graph.

Step 3: Locate the data and do the math.

Data Interpretation Practice Question

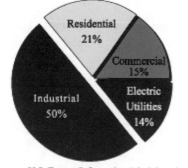

NATURAL GAS CONSUMPTION IN THE UNITED STATES IN 2003

Source: U.S. Energy Information Administration

6. Based on this graph, for every 1,000 barrels of natural gas consumed by residential users, approximately how many barrels are consumed by electric utilities?

(A) 140
(B) 667
(C) 700
(D) 750
(E) 1,400

Paired Data Interpretation

NATURAL GAS CONSUMPTION IN THE UNITED STATES IN 2003

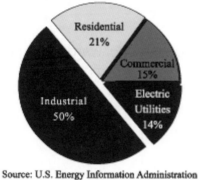

Source: U.S. Energy Information Administration

7. If residential users consumed approximately 1.4 trillion more cubic feet of natural gas than commercial users did in 2003, which of the following comes closest to the total natural gas consumption in the United States that year, in cubic feet?

(A) 8 trillion
(B) 21 trillion
(C) 23 trillion
(D) 29 trillion
(E) 38 trillion

Summary

In this unit, you learned that:

- reading the question again helps to make sure you answer the question asked.

- you can translate English into math.

- you can use translation, plugging in, or working backwards to answer word problems.

- data interpretation problems are not that scary.

Answer Key

1. 40
2. 8
3. E
4. D
5. C
6. B
7. C

Session 4: SAT Grammar I

In this unit, you will learn to:

- master common grammar concepts tested on the SAT.

- recognize common SAT grammar mistakes.

- solve typical SAT grammar questions.

Verb Tense

Verb tenses show when something happened—in the past, the present, or the future. On the SAT, you'll need to recognize the forms of verbs that should (or shouldn't) be used in various types of sentences.

Verb Tense Tested in Sentence Improvement

1. The students organized themselves into small groups, <u>which helps them</u> to divide up the work and finish their studying more quickly.

(A) which helps them
(B) that was helping them
(C) helpful to them
(D) which helped them
(E) thus being helpful to them

Verb Tense Tested in Error Identification

2. <u>After years of</u> hard work, <u>including writing letters</u> and
       A   B

holding events, the group has <u>finally began</u> to <u>spread its</u>
                                    C   D

message to the public. <u>No error</u>
                             E

Be wary of the most complicated answer choices in verb tense questions. They usually are not correct.

Subject-Verb Agreement

They [go / goes] to the store.

Which verb is correct? Why?

Common Trap 1: Distracting Phrases

Circle the noun and verb in the sentence below, and underline the phrase that comes between them.

The robot, which is made of many parts, break often.

Read the sentence without the unnecessary phrase. Is it correct?

Common Trap 2: Tricky Singular Nouns

Of the nouns below, which are singular, and which are plural?

neither   none   team   series   group

Circle the correct verb in each sentence below.

Neither of my brothers [is / are] going to the party.

None of my shirts [is / are] blue.

The team [was / were] on a winning streak.

The lecture series [starts / start] next week.

Each group [has / have] five minutes to solve the problem.

Some singular nouns are easily mistaken for plural. Become familiar with and watch out for common tricky singular nouns like the ones above.

Note: Photocopying any part of this book is prohibited by law.

115

Pronouns

Pronouns replace nouns in ways that should be familiar to you. Suppose that a man named Henry made each of the following statements. Which common pronouns would replace his name in each sentence?

> Henry saw the man.
> The man saw Henry.
> That is Henry's.

Common Trap 1: Complex Sentences

> Bryan asked Ann and I to go the park with him.

Complex sentences make it difficult to identify errors. Can you simplify the sentence above? Does it sound correct in its simplified form?

Common Trap 2: Singular vs. Plural Pronouns

What is the pronoun in the sentence below? Is it correct?

> The convenience of drive-through windows accounts for its popularity.

Which of the subjects below should be replaced with he or she, and which should be replaced with they?

> Each player   All the girls   No one   Our families

Whenever you see an underlined pronoun on the SAT, ask yourself what noun the pronoun replaces. Look for mismatched pronouns or pronouns that don't clearly refer to any particular noun.

Note: Photocopying any part of this book is prohibited by law.

116

Practice Questions: Set 1

Use the concepts you've learned so far to solve these practice questions.

3. After our band had been <u>practicing</u> for weeks, we
                                         A

<u>noticed that</u> the number of mistakes we made <u>were</u>
   B   C

<u>growing smaller</u>. <u>No error</u>
      D   E

4. We tried to figure out whether the car slid <u>because the driver was going too fast, or because the road having a layer of ice.</u>

(A) because the driver was going too fast, or because the road having a layer of ice
(B) because the driver goes too fast, or because the road having a layer of ice
(C) because of the driver going too fast, or for having a layer of ice
(D) as a result of the driver, which was going too fast, or as a result of the road, having a layer of ice
(E) because the driver was going too fast, or because the road had a layer of ice

5. <u>Everybody took their seat</u> as the speaker cleared his throat for attention and prepared to begin the lecture.

(A) Everybody took their seat
(B) Everybody taking a seat
(C) Everybody took his or her seat
(D) All the people taking seats
(E) All people to take a seat

Modifiers

A modifier is a word or phrase that describes something in a sentence. The simplest modifiers are adjectives and adverbs, while others are made up of several words. Can you identify the modifier in each sentence below?

> The hot sun shone.
> She ran quickly.
> Always willing to lend a hand, Harry is a great friend.

Common Trap 1: Misplaced Modifiers

Identify the modifier in the sentence below, and see if you can find a better place for it.

> Decorated with candles and pink icing, the baker served the cake.

Pay particular attention to lengthy modifying phrases. It is common to mistakenly separate such phrases from the things they modify.

Common Trap 2: Dangling Modifiers

Identify the modifier in the sentence below. What does it modify?

> A great improvement, the mayor approved the new policy.

Dangling modifiers usually come at the beginning of the sentence. Take note when a sentence begins with a descriptive phrase that is followed by a comma. You'll know the sentence contains a dangling modifier if the description before the comma doesn't match the noun that comes right after the comma.

Modifiers: Practice

Can you identify the dangling or misplaced modifier in each sentence? How would you fix it?

Having eaten lunch, it was time for a nap.

Swinging from trapezes, the audience members watched the acrobats.

Bright and colorful, the artist painted scenes of nature.

The hat sat on top of the woman's head, which was enormous.

Headlines

Mistakes in grammar can suggest some very interesting but incorrect interpretations.

What do the following headlines mean to say? What do they actually say?

Miners Refuse to Work After Death

Two Sisters Reunite After Eighteen Years at Checkout Counter

Two Soviet Ships Collide – One Dies

Enraged Cow Injures Farmer with Axe

Squad Helps Dog Bite Victim

Grandmother of Eight Makes Hole in One

Parallelism

Parallelism means that similar parts of a sentence match each other.

Parallel Verbs

What's wrong with the sentence below? Can you form two grammatically correct rewrites?

> I like swimming, dancing, and to sing.

Parallel Pronouns

What's wrong with the following sentence? Come up with a grammatically correct rewrite.

> If you try hard enough, one can usually succeed.

Keep an eye out for sentences that feel unbalanced. Check to see that verbs in a list are written in the same tense, and that pronouns that refer to the same noun match each other.

Pay particular attention to word endings. For example, if two items in a list end in "-ing," the third item should end in "-ing" as well.

Note: Photocopying any part of this book is prohibited by law.

120

Practice Questions: Set 2

Use the concepts you've learned so far to solve these practice questions.

6. The movie <u>contains</u> a surprising twist in the middle—viewers
          A

expecting a <u>predictable</u> romantic comedy <u>will find</u> themselves
          B   C

<u>to watch</u> an entirely different film. <u>No error</u>
  D   E

7. <u>There are</u> two reasons that the <u>business is</u> doing so
    A   B

well: first, it has <u>excellent employees,</u> <u>and plus</u> it sells
                     C   D

high-quality products. <u>No error</u>
                    E

8. <u>A great honor, Mr. Jones received the Teacher of the Year Award</u> for his excellent work.

(A) A great honor, Mr. Jones received the Teacher of the Year Award
(B) Mr. Jones received the Teacher of the Year Award, a great honor,
(C) Mr. Jones, receiving the Teacher of the Year Award a great honor,
(D) To receive the Teacher of the Year Award a great honor, Mr. Jones
(E) A great honor was receiving the Teacher of the Year Award, Mr. Jones

Summary

In this unit, you leaned that:

- a subject and its verb must agree for a sentence to be grammatically correct.

- you can eliminate unnecessary phrases to make it easier to check for subject-verb agreement.

- modifiers should go next to the words they modify.

- you can simplify sentences to check for proper pronoun usage.

- the parts of a sentence should be parallel.

Answer Key

1. D
2. C
3. C
4. E
5. C
6. D
7. D
8. B

Note: Photocopying any part of this book is prohibited by law.

122

Session 5: Arithmetic Fundamentals

In this unit, you will:

- learn to recognize the major arithmetic concepts tested on the SAT.

- review the basics of SAT arithmetic concepts.

- practice on questions based on SAT arithmetic concepts.

Note: Photocopying any part of this book is prohibited by law.

123

Mean

Mean is another word for average. We use the idea of averages every day, for things like figuring out your grade in a class. It's basically a way to get a summary of a lot of different numbers.

Let's say you got the following test scores in your math class:

76
82
88
92

To find the average of these scores (which would tell you your final grade in the class), you need to find the total of the scores.

The total of the scores is _____.

Then divide the total by the number of scores you received. There were four scores, so divide the total by four.

The result is _____. This is the average of the scores.

The equation to solve an average question is

total of the items = (number of items)(average of the items).

A great way to organize the numbers when figuring out averages is to use the average T.

1. Four area shelters have the following number of pets available for adoption: 19, 25, 30, and 34. What is the average (arithmetic mean) number of pets available for adoption at the four shelters?

(A) 19
(B) 22
(C) 25
(D) 27
(E) 27.5

2. A troop of scouts sold an average of 56 bars of candy each during their annual fund drive. If the scouts sold a total of 1,904 candy bars, how many scouts are in the troop?

(A) 18
(B) 22
(C) 27
(D) 29
(E) 34

3. What is the average of the set of integers $\{n, n + 1, n + 3, n + 4\}$?

(A) $4n + 8$
(B) $4n + 2$
(C) $2n$
(D) $n + 2$
(E) $4n \div 2$

4. If the average of five numbers is 12, and the average of two of these numbers is 15, what is the average of the remaining three numbers?

(A) 7
(B) 8
(C) 10
(D) 12
(E) 14

Medians and Modes

Median

The median of a set of numbers is the middle number, when the numbers are in consecutive order.

The median of the set of numbers {3, 3, 7, 39, 400} is _____.

The median of the set of numbers {4, 6,8,12} is _____.

The median of the set of numbers {13, 15, 4, 22, 18, 22} is _____.

5. For which of the following sets is the median equal to the mean?

(A) {2, 5, 9, 12, 13}
(B) {3, 4, 8, 12, 13}
(C) {2, 6, 10, 12, 14}
(D) {3, 4, 9, 11, 13}
(E) {3, 5, 10, 11, 12}

Mode

The mode of a set of numbers is the number that appears most often.

The mode of the set of numbers {6, 6, 9, 9, 9, 14, 16, 16, 25} is _____.

The mode of the set of numbers {4, 7, 19, 8, 4, 12, 9, 8} is _____.

6. For which of the following sets is the mean greater than the mode and the mode greater than the median?

(A) {6, 8, 11, 44, 44, 3000}
(B) {14, 14, 19, 20}
(C) {1, 2, 3, 4, 5, 5, 8}
(D) {5, 7, 7, 351}
(E) {−4, 0, 4, 4}

Converting Ratios and Numbers

A ratio is a way of comparing two numbers.

"The ratio of x to y" can be written as $x : y$ or $\dfrac{x}{y}$.

- 7 to 2 is not the same as 2 to 7.

- Ratios compare like quantities.

- Ratios compare quantities with uniform units.

- Ratios should be in simplest form.

A classroom contains 20 boys and 15 girls. What is the ratio of:

- boys to girls?

- girls to boys?

- boys to total number of children?

- girls to total number of children?

Sometimes you're given the ratio, and you need to find the number.

If the ratio of owls to eagles is 4 : 5, and there are 12 owls

- How many eagles are there?

- How many birds are there?

7. In a certain parking lot, there are 24 cars and 15 trucks. If there are no other vehicles in the lot, what is the ratio of cars to trucks in the lot?

(A) 5 : 8
(B) 5 : 13
(C) 8 : 5
(D) 8 : 13
(E) 15 : 24

8. If the ratio of juniors to seniors is 6 : 5, then which of the following could be the number of juniors?

(A) 25
(B) 28
(C) 33
(D) 36
(E) 40

9. If a jar contains 14 red marbles and 9 blue marbles, what will be the ratio of blue marbles to red marbles after one third of the blue marbles are removed?

(A) 9 : 14
(B) 14 : 9
(C) 7 : 3
(D) 3 : 7
(E) 3 : 10

10. A jewelry designer needs to cut a length of wire into two pieces that form a ratio of 4:5. If the length of wire is 72 inches long, how long, in inches, will the smaller piece be?

(A) 8
(B) 9
(C) 32
(D) 36
(E) 40

Note: Photocopying any part of this book is prohibited by law.

128

Rates

A rate is a sort of ratio. The word "per" is a giveaway: It means you're dealing with a rate.

Rates can be expressed as fractions. Put one thing on top of the other:

$$\frac{distance}{time} \qquad \frac{cost}{mile}$$

To solve a rates question, set up two fractions, and make them equal to each other. On one side, put the fraction with information you know. On the other side of the equal sign put the fraction with information you're looking for.

If Angel buys 5 apples for 40 cents, how many apples can she buy for $1.20?

$$\frac{5}{40} = \frac{x}{120}$$

Now solve.

11. At a stationery store, ball-point pens cost $2.75 for a box of 12. How much will Elmer need to spend if he wants to buy 60 ball-point pens?

(A) $0.55
(B) $13.75
(C) $33.00
(D) $165.00
(E) $720.00

Note: Photocopying any part of this book is prohibited by law.

129

12. The pastry chefs at Betty's Bakery bake 25 apple pies every two hours. If they maintain this constant rate over the course of a 10-hour workday, how many apple pies will they bake?

(A) 25
(B) 50
(C) 100
(D) 125
(E) 250

13. Kelly drove 120 miles in 90 minutes. If Kelly maintained a constant speed, how many minutes did it take her to drive 80 miles?

(A) 6
(B) 10.7
(C) 44.3
(D) 50
(E) 60

14. If it took Audrey 3 hours working at a constant rate to complete her book report, what part of the report was finished during the first 30 minutes?

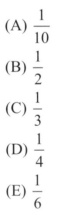

(A) $\dfrac{1}{10}$

(B) $\dfrac{1}{2}$

(C) $\dfrac{1}{3}$

(D) $\dfrac{1}{4}$

(E) $\dfrac{1}{6}$

Before you start writing fractions, what do you have to do with the time units in this problem?

15. When Denise walks her dog, she walks at a constant rate of $\frac{1}{2}$ mile per hour. If she walked her dog last night for 15 minutes, how far, in miles, did she and her dog walk?

(A) $\frac{1}{8}$

(B) $\frac{1}{2}$

(C) 2

(D) $7\frac{1}{2}$

(E) 8

Percents

If "per" means you're dealing with a rate, and "cent" means one hundred, what does "percent" mean?

Olivia got 8 out of 10 questions right. What percent did Olivia get right?

Since percents are ratios, you can set up ratios to help you solve percent questions. Set up the ratio in the form of a fraction. Then use your calculator to solve the fraction.

We ate 2 of the 7 pies we bought on Friday. What percent of the pies we bought did we eat?

Set up the ratio in the form of a fraction:

Now use your calculator to solve:

What percent of the pies we bought did we NOT eat?

Note: Photocopying any part of this book is prohibited by law.

132

16. There are 300 apples in a barrel, and 60 of these apples are bruised. What percent of the apples are bruised?

(A) 10%
(B) 20%
(C) 30%
(D) 40%
(E) 60%

17. What percent of 3 is 4?

(A) 25%
(B) 33%
(C) 75%
(D) 125%
(E) 133%

18. If 25% of 50% of x is 10, what is x percent of 50?

(A) 25
(B) 40
(C) 75
(D) 200
(E) 400

Probabilities

Probabilities, like percentages and rates, are a type of ratio.

Probabilities express:

$$\frac{\text{The chance of a certain event happening}}{\text{The total number of events possible}}$$

For example, if there are 10 socks in a drawer, and 3 of them are yellow, 10 is the "total number of events possible" (the total number of socks). 3 is the "chance of a certain event happening" (since you're interested in knowing the probability of choosing a yellow sock).

The way to express the probability that you will choose a yellow sock out of the drawer is $\frac{3}{10}$, or 30%.

If you roll a regular 6-sided die, what is the probability that you will roll a 4?

What is the total number of events possible in this question?

What is the chance of rolling a 4?

How do you express this as a probability?

If you flip a coin, what is the probability of getting heads?

19. In Candice's drawer, there are 7 black shirts, 12 blue shirts, and 6 gray shirts. Choosing one randomly, what is the probability of Candice pulling out a gray shirt from the drawer?

(A) 6%
(B) 12%
(C) 19%
(D) 20%
(E) 24%

20. If the numbers 1 through 9 are written on individual slips of paper and put into a jar, what is the probability that a person drawing one slip of paper out of the jar will draw an even number?

(A) 11.1%
(B) 12.5%
(C) 40%
(D) 44.4%
(E) 50%

Summary

In this unit, you learned that:

- mean (average) is calculated by dividing the total of the items by the number of items.

- median is the middle number of a set of numbers and mode is the most frequently-occurring number in a set of numbers.

- you should calculate a ratio as a fraction and then reduce it.

- you should set up a proportion to turn a ratio into an actual number.

- you should write rates as fractions and solve them by setting up proportions.

- percents can be calculated by setting up a fraction and converting it with your calculator.

- the two parts necessary to calculate a probability are the total possible events and the chance of a certain event happening.

Answer Key

1. D
2. E
3. D
4. C
5. B
6. A
7. C
8. D
9. D
10. C
11. B
12. D
13. E
14. E
15. A
16. B
17. E
18. B
19. E
20. D

Session 5: Answering Reading Questions

In this unit, you will learn:

- to recognize common Critical Reading passage-based question types.

- how to approach the different question types.

- to distinguish question types that require you to read the whole passage from those that provide a specific line reference.

The Three Major Question Types

These are the most common types of passage-based questions that you'll find in the SAT Critical Reading section.

- Detail
- Inference
- "Why"

Detail Questions

Detail questions ask about specific things the author says in the passage. They test whether or not you understand the information in the passage.

Many Detail questions have specific wording.

> The segment of the speech the audience appreciated most was...

Some Detail questions contain clues.

> The passage indicates that...

> According to the author...

> The author argues that...

> The author characterizes (something) as...

To solve Detail questions:

(1) Go back to the passage and locate the information you need to answer the question.
(2) Read the relevant information.
(3) Keep your eye out for common wrong answer choices.

Inference Questions

Inference questions ask you to read between the lines. To answer these questions, you must figure out what the author thinks or means, but doesn't directly say.

Some Inference questions contain clues.

The **author suggests that**...

The **author implies that**...

The **passage suggests/implies that**...

In the context of the passage, the **phrase** "(from the passage)" **suggests that**...

To solve Inference questions:

(1) Reread the relevant information in the passage.
(2) Focus on what the section means in the context of the passage.
(3) Combine statements when possible.
(4) Beware of choices that refer to but distort specific information in the passage.
(5) Make sure there is evidence to support your choice.

"Why?" Questions

"Why?" questions ask you to recognize the reasons why examples, quotations, and other writing elements appear in the passage.

"Why?" questions can appear in the following forms:

The author **mentions** (something) **in order to**...

The author **uses the word** (something) in line 10 **in order to make the point that**...

The **reference to** (something) in line 23 **serves to**...

In line 17, the **author mentions** (something) **to illustrate that**...

To solve "Why?" questions:

(1) Use the line reference to go to the text in question.
(2) Try to determine why the author uses that example, word, or phrase.
(3) Look at the answer choices, searching for one that comes close to your reason.
(4) Beware of choices that distort or are outside the scope of the passage.

Because of its enormous size, the United States is a country of contrasts. Nowhere are the differences between the eastern and western United States as profound as in climate and availability of water.

The eastern and western United States differ in many ways, but perhaps the most significant difference between the two areas is climate. The East receives enough rainfall to sustain agriculture, while the West does not receive adequate rainfall to do so. Additionally, the West has smaller regions with widely disparate climatic variations. The mountains, the
5 Sierra Nevadas and the Cascades, that impede the Pacific Ocean's ability to cool in the summer and warm in the winter, and that block the fronts that bring moisture in the form of rain and snow, have much to do with the extremes of climate found in the West. Elevations in the interior West also affect climate because even the mountainous flatlands have elevations higher than a mile.
10 Because of these extremes, particularly in the area of rainfall (there can be as much as 150 inches of precipitation annually on the western side of the Sierra-Cascade range as contrasted with as little as four inches annually on the eastern side), irrigation becomes critical if the area is to remain viable for human habitation. It is so hot in some portions of the western desert that, even when rain clouds form, the earth's reflected heat dissipates most of the moisture
15 before it can reach the ground. Any drops that actually reach the ground quickly evaporate. The arid Central Plains of the United States can use water for irrigation from the Ogallala Aquifer, a closed-basin aquifer discovered after World War I. The western regions, however, are too far away to benefit from this trapped run-off from several Ice Ages that is confined in gravel beds stretching from South Dakota to West Texas. No wonder then that water is so
20 precious to the people and farmlands of the West and that the population of this area continually presses for national, state, and local funding for irrigation projects that will store and reroute water for them.
The Colorado River, with its various tributaries, including the Gunnison, the Green, and the Gila, has long been the source of most irrigation projects in the desert areas of the West.
25 Much of the water from the Colorado River goes into the state of California to irrigate the Imperial and San Joaquin Valleys. On its route from high in the Rockies to the Gulf of California, the river is diverted in many areas to irrigate fields. Unfortunately, when it returns after having passed through deposits of mineral salts in the soil that was irrigated, the salinity of the water has increased dramatically. The amount of salt in the water can then have a
30 detrimental effect on the crops if proper drainage systems are not built. Not only is a proper drainage system exorbitantly expensive, but drainage systems create run-off, which must be handled in some efficient way. By the time the water is drained, this run-off not only contains salt, but probably pesticides as well, and the question of what to do with the run-off becomes an issue.
35 Despite the years of better-than-average rainfall in the late 70s and early to mid-80s that even caused the Great Salt Lake in Utah to flood, the situation in the western desert areas, particularly California, remains critical. It is not uncommon for droughts in the state to last several years. Consequently, water, not only for crops, but for human consumption itself, is at stake. Thus, it is a serious mandate to solve this area's water problem if the area is to survive.

Detail Practice Questions

1. The extreme heat in some parts of the western desert (lines 13-15)

(A) prevents the formation of clouds over those areas of the desert
(B) periodically disrupts cultural events planned in the region
(C) stops all rain from reaching the ground
(D) impedes significant accumulation of moisture in the area
(E) prevents water from the Ogallala Aquifer from reaching the area

2. The first paragraph is primarily concerned with

(A) differences between the eastern and western United States
(B) factors affecting climate in the western United States
(C) the mountains of the western United States
(D) variations in climate in the eastern United States
(E) the way in which rainfall influences a region's agriculture

Inference Practice Questions

3. The effect of the Sierra Nevadas and the Cascades, as discussed in lines 4-7, suggests that

(A) large bodies of water can affect the climate of a region
(B) the Sierra Nevadas and the Cascades do not influence the climate of the west
(C) these mountain ranges receive no rain or snow
(D) the west experiences mild winters
(E) the Sierra Nevadas and the Cascades have a greater effect on climate than do the mountainous flatlands in the interior

4. The discussion in paragraph 3 suggests that the author would most likely agree with which of the following statements?

(A) California receives more than its fair share of the water available from the Colorado River.
(B) The Gunnison, Green, and Gila tributaries are responsible for most of the water used to irrigate the Western deserts.
(C) The cost of a solution should be the primary consideration in determining whether that solution should be implemented.
(D) Crop damage is inevitable once the salinity level of irrigation water increases dramatically.
(E) It is possible for the solution of one problem to create a new problem.

Note: Photocopying any part of this book is prohibited by law.

141

Because of its enormous size, the United States is a country of contrasts. Nowhere are the differences between the eastern and western United States as profound as in climate and availability of water.

The eastern and western United States differ in many ways, but perhaps the most significant difference between the two areas is climate. The East receives enough rainfall to sustain agriculture, while the West does not receive adequate rainfall to do so. Additionally, the West has smaller regions with widely disparate climatic variations. The mountains, the
5   Sierra Nevadas and the Cascades, that impede the Pacific Ocean's ability to cool in the summer and warm in the winter, and that block the fronts that bring moisture in the form of rain and snow, have much to do with the extremes of climate found in the West. Elevations in the interior West also affect climate because even the mountainous flatlands have elevations higher than a mile.
10   Because of these extremes, particularly in the area of rainfall (there can be as much as 150 inches of precipitation annually on the western side of the Sierra-Cascade range as contrasted with as little as four inches annually on the eastern side), irrigation becomes critical if the area is to remain viable for human habitation. It is so hot in some portions of the western desert that, even when rain clouds form, the earth's reflected heat dissipates most of the moisture
15   before it can reach the ground. Any drops that actually reach the ground quickly evaporate. The arid Central Plains of the United States can use water for irrigation from the Ogallala Aquifer, a closed-basin aquifer discovered after World War I. The western regions, however, are too far away to benefit from this trapped run-off from several Ice Ages that is confined in gravel beds stretching from South Dakota to West Texas. No wonder then that water is so
20   precious to the people and farmlands of the West and that the population of this area continually presses for national, state, and local funding for irrigation projects that will store and reroute water for them.
The Colorado River, with its various tributaries, including the Gunnison, the Green, and the Gila, has long been the source of most irrigation projects in the desert areas of the West.
25   Much of the water from the Colorado River goes into the state of California to irrigate the Imperial and San Joaquin Valleys. On its route from high in the Rockies to the Gulf of California, the river is diverted in many areas to irrigate fields. Unfortunately, when it returns after having passed through deposits of mineral salts in the soil that was irrigated, the salinity of the water has increased dramatically. The amount of salt in the water can then have a
30   detrimental effect on the crops if proper drainage systems are not built. Not only is a proper drainage system exorbitantly expensive, but drainage systems create run-off, which must be handled in some efficient way. By the time the water is drained, this run-off not only contains salt, but probably pesticides as well, and the question of what to do with the run-off becomes an issue.
35   Despite the years of better-than-average rainfall in the late 70s and early to mid-80s that even caused the Great Salt Lake in Utah to flood, the situation in the western desert areas, particularly California, remains critical. It is not uncommon for droughts in the state to last several years. Consequently, water, not only for crops, but for human consumption itself, is at stake. Thus, it is a serious mandate to solve this area's water problem if the area is to survive.

Why? Practice Questions

5. In lines 16-17, the author mentions the Ogallala Aquifer primarily to

(A) provide an example of a closed-basin aquifer
(B) dismiss the claim that irrigation funding is necessary for the Central Plains of the United States
(C) illustrate a disadvantage the West faces with respect to acquiring sufficient water
(D) demonstrate the method by which raindrops evaporate
(E) argue that the drought problem in the West is not as severe as some contend

6. In the context of the passage, the phrase "that even caused the Great Salt Lake in Utah to flood" (lines 35-36) primarily serves to

(A) dispute the claim that the West experienced better than average rainfall in the 1970s and 1980s
(B) single out California as the area most greatly in need of water
(C) illustrate that droughts can last for several years
(D) provide evidence for a factor that could have, but did not, solve the irrigation problem in the West
(E) present flooding as a significant problem in the West

Other Question Types

In addition to the three most common question types, you can expect to see a few other types.

- Primary Purpose/Main Point
- Vocabulary-in-Context
- Tone

The following pages contain examples of each.

Primary Purpose/Main Point Questions

Primary Purpose/Main Point questions ask about the meaning of the passage as a whole. Main Idea questions ask about the passage by itself while Primary Purpose questions ask about how the author gets that point across.

Consider the following answer choices:

George Washington was a talented military general despite having lost most battles in the Revolutionary War.

This choice could serve as the answer to a _____ question.

to demonstrate that George Washington was an astute military general despite having lost most battles in the Revolutionary War

This choice could serve as the answer to a _____ question.

To solve Primary Purpose/Main Point questions:

(1) Read the whole passage before you answer.
(2) Try to answer without looking back at the passage.
(3) Beware of choices that distort the passage's overall orientation.
(4) Put yourself in the place of the author.

Note: Photocopying any part of this book is prohibited by law.

144

Vocabulary-in-Context Questions

Vocabulary-in-Context questions ask you to recognize the meaning of a word as it is used in a sentence in the passage. These questions always come with a line reference that directs you to the word's location in the passage.

Vocabulary-in-Context questions usually look like this:

In line 25, "intrepid" **most nearly means**...

The word "malevolent" **as it is used** in line 45 **most nearly means**...

To solve Vocabulary-in-Context questions:

(1) Use the line reference to go to the word in question.
(2) Read a sentence or two before and after the word.
(3) Come up with a word that could replace the word.
(4) Eliminate choices that don't fit.
(5) To test the remaining choices, read them back into the sentence in place of the original word.
(6) Beware of common synonyms of the word that do not match the word's meaning in the passage.

Tone Questions

Tone questions ask about the mood or attitude of the author or, occasionally, the attitude of some character mentioned in the passage.

Tone questions usually look like this:

The **tone** of the passage **is primarily one of**...

A more specific Tone question might look like this:

The **author's attitude toward** (something the author mentions) **is best described as**...

To solve Tone questions:

(1) Locate the issue in the passage and summarize the author's or character's mood about it.
(2) Decide whether the tone or attitude is positive, negative, or neutral.
(3) Eliminate all choices that don't match the overall tone you chose (positive, negative, or neutral).
(4) Select from the remaining choices the one that comes closest to capturing the tone or attitude as you see it.

Because of its enormous size, the United States is a country of contrasts. Nowhere are the differences between the eastern and western United States as profound as in climate and availability of water.

The eastern and western United States differ in many ways, but perhaps the most significant difference between the two areas is climate. The East receives enough rainfall to sustain agriculture, while the West does not receive adequate rainfall to do so. Additionally, the West has smaller regions with widely disparate climatic variations. The mountains, the
5 Sierra Nevadas and the Cascades, that impede the Pacific Ocean's ability to cool in the summer and warm in the winter, and that block the fronts that bring moisture in the form of rain and snow, have much to do with the extremes of climate found in the West. Elevations in the interior West also affect climate because even the mountainous flatlands have elevations higher than a mile.
10 Because of these extremes, particularly in the area of rainfall (there can be as much as 150 inches of precipitation annually on the western side of the Sierra-Cascade range as contrasted with as little as four inches annually on the eastern side), irrigation becomes critical if the area is to remain viable for human habitation. It is so hot in some portions of the western desert that, even when rain clouds form, the earth's reflected heat dissipates most of the moisture
15 before it can reach the ground. Any drops that actually reach the ground quickly evaporate. The arid Central Plains of the United States can use water for irrigation from the Ogallala Aquifer, a closed-basin aquifer discovered after World War I. The western regions, however, are too far away to benefit from this trapped run-off from several Ice Ages that is confined in gravel beds stretching from South Dakota to West Texas. No wonder then that water is so
20 precious to the people and farmlands of the West and that the population of this area continually presses for national, state, and local funding for irrigation projects that will store and reroute water for them.

    The Colorado River, with its various tributaries, including the Gunnison, the Green, and the Gila, has long been the source of most irrigation projects in the desert areas of the West.
25 Much of the water from the Colorado River goes into the state of California to irrigate the Imperial and San Joaquin Valleys. On its route from high in the Rockies to the Gulf of California, the river is diverted in many areas to irrigate fields. Unfortunately, when it returns after having passed through deposits of mineral salts in the soil that was irrigated, the salinity of the water has increased dramatically. The amount of salt in the water can then have a
30 detrimental effect on the crops if proper drainage systems are not built. Not only is a proper drainage system exorbitantly expensive, but drainage systems create run-off, which must be handled in some efficient way. By the time the water is drained, this run-off not only contains salt, but probably pesticides as well, and the question of what to do with the run-off becomes an issue.
35 Despite the years of better-than-average rainfall in the late 70s and early to mid-80s that even caused the Great Salt Lake in Utah to flood, the situation in the western desert areas, particularly California, remains critical. It is not uncommon for droughts in the state to last several years. Consequently, water, not only for crops, but for human consumption itself, is at stake. Thus, it is a serious mandate to solve this area's water problem if the area is to survive.

Primary Purpose/Main Point Practice Question

7. The author's primary purpose in the passage is to

(A) describe the differences in climate between the eastern and western United States
(B) demonstrate that the water shortage in the western United States is the greatest problem facing the country today
(C) argue that a solution to the water problem is necessary if certain areas of the western United States are to remain suitable for living
(D) dismiss the notion that there are no significant climatic differences between the eastern and western United States
(E) discuss the role of the Colorado River in irrigating the areas of the western United States

Vocabulary-in-Context Practice Question

8. In line 3, "sustain" most nearly means

(A) prolong
(B) implement
(C) support
(D) defend
(E) confirm

Tone Practice Question

9. The tone of the passage is primarily one of

(A) utter resignation
(B) unwavering confidence
(C) hysterical alarm
(D) mild indifference
(E) serious concern

Summary

In this unit, you learned that:

- the three main passage-based question types are Detail questions, Inference questions, and "Why?" questions.

- other question types include Primary Purpose/Main Point questions, Vocabulary-in-Context questions, and Tone questions.

- many questions, including Detail questions and Vocabulary-in-Context questions, supply a line number.

- Primary Purpose/Main Point questions and Tone questions are more general, asking about the passage as a whole.

- Inference questions ask you to read between the lines.

Answer Key

1. D
2. B
3. A
4. E
5. C
6. D
7. C
8. C
9. E

Note: Photocopying any part of this book is prohibited by law.

148

Session 6: Geometry Fundamentals I

In this unit, you will learn to:

- apply your knowledge of properties of angles, lines, and common geometric figures to questions.

- answer questions based on the characteristics of the angles and sides of a triangle.

- recognize different quadrilaterals and their properties.

- find the side lengths, angle measures, perimeters, and areas of triangles and quadrilaterals.

Lines and Angles

Some SAT geometry questions revolve around the fact that since there are 180 degrees in a straight line, angles that share a line add up to 180.

The following figure shows five angles sharing a line.

What is the sum of these five angles? _____

What equation represents this relationship? _____

What is the value of a? _____

Vertical Angles

Whenever two lines intersect, two pairs of vertical angles are formed. The vertical angles are the angles that lie opposite each other, and they are always equal to each other.

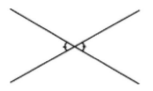

Look at the figure below. Mark the angle that is vertical to angle *v* on the diagram.

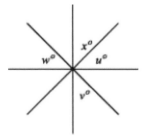

What relationship does the angle that you just marked have with angles *w*, *x* and *u*?

_____

What is the value of *u* + *v* + *w* + *x*? _____

Degrees in a Circle

Just as there are always 360° in a circle, there are always 360° in angles around a point.

When working with angles around a point, you can determine the measure of an unknown angle by subtracting the measures of the known angles from 360°.

If the angles around a point measure 70, 50, 120, 60 and x, what is the value of x? _____

Look at the following figure. What is the value of y? _____

Note: Photocopying any part of this book is prohibited by law.

152

Parallel Lines

When a line (transversal) crosses parallel lines to create large and small angles:

- every large angle has the same degree measure as every other large angle.
- every small angle has the same degree measure as every other small angle.
- the measure of any large angle plus the measure of any small angle equals 180 degrees.

Look at the following figure.

$l \| m$

Is the angle measuring y a small angle or a large angle?

_____

Is the angle measuring $4y$ a small angle or a large angle?

_____

What is the relationship between the angle measuring y and the angle measuring 4y?

_____

What is the value of y?

_____

Lines and Angles: Practice Questions

Here are two examples of how lines and angles might be tested on the SAT.

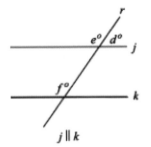

1. In the figure above, what is the value of $a + b$?

(A) 60
(B) 90
(C) 120
(D) 140
(E) 180

2. In the figure above, if the value of f is 120, what is the value of d?

(A) 25
(B) 50
(C) 60
(D) 90
(E) 120

Triangles

Triangles are the most common type of geometric figure found on the SAT. Here's what you need to know:

Triangle Angle Measures

- A triangle is a figure with three sides and three angles.
- The sum of the angle measures of any triangle, regardless of how big, how small, how fat or how skinny, is always 180°.

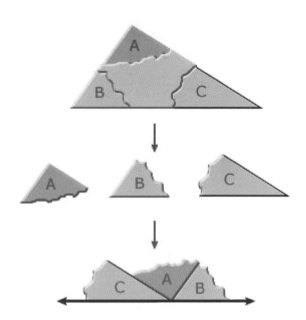

Note: Photocopying any part of this book is prohibited by law.

155

If You Know Two, You Can Find the Third

When you know the measures of two of a triangle's angles, you can figure out the measure of the third by subtracting the sum of the other two angles from 180.

$a + b + c = 180.$

If two of a triangle's angles measure 35° and 95°, what does the third angle measure?

_____

If two of a triangle's angles measure x and y, what does the third angle measure in terms of x and y?

_____

Area of a Triangle

The formula for the area (A) of a triangle is: $\frac{1}{2}bh$.

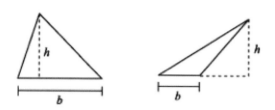

What is the area of a triangle with $b = 2$ and $h = 3$?

_____

If the area of a triangle is 12 and its height measures 4, what does its base measure?

_____

Pythagorean Theorem

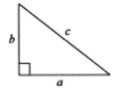

The Pythagorean Theorem states:

$$a^2 + b^2 = c^2,$$

where a and b are the two shorter sides (or legs) of a right triangle and c is the longest side (or hypotenuse).

For example, if the two legs of a right triangle are 3 and 4, the hypotenuse must be: _____

So, if the two legs of a right triangle are 12 and 5, what is the length of the hypotenuse?

_____

What is the area of a right triangle with legs of length 12 and 5?
_____.

If you know that the hypotenuse of a right triangle is 10 and one of the legs is 6, what is the measure of the other leg?

_____

Triangle Inequality Theorem

If you know the lengths of two of the three sides of a triangle, you can figure out a range of possible lengths for the third side.

The third side must be shorter than the sum of the other two sides. Can you explain why?

_____

The third side must be longer than the difference of the other two sides. Can you explain why?

_____

If two sides of a triangle have lengths 3 and 5, then the length of the third side has to be between what two numbers? _____ and _____

Can the following sets of sides be the sides of a triangle? Why or why not?

3, 5 and 9 _____

4, 5 and 6 _____

2, 4 and 7 _____

Triangles: Practice Questions

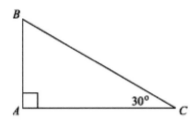

3. In the triangle above, what is the measure of angle *B*?

_____

4. What is the area, in square units, of a right triangle with a leg of length 6 and a hypotenuse of length 10?

(A) 12
(B) 24
(C) 30
(D) 48
(E) 60

Quadrilaterals

All quadrilaterals have two things in common: they have four straight sides, and the measures of their interior angles add up to 360 degrees.

So, if three angles of a quadrilateral measured 120, 60, and 80, what would the measure of the fourth angle be?

_____

The following quadrilateral types appear on the SAT:

Parallelograms

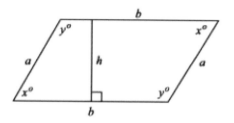

A parallelogram is a quadrilateral (four-sided figure) with two pairs of parallel sides.

- A parallelogram's opposite sides are equal.

- A parallelogram's opposite angles are equal.

- The measures of any two consecutive (non-opposite) angles add up to 180 degrees. So, in this figure, $x + y = 180$.

If each of two angles of a parallelogram measure 80, what do the two remaining angles measure?

_____ and _____.

Rectangles

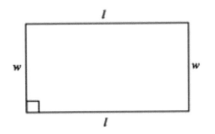

A rectangle is a parallelogram with four right angles.
A rectangle's opposite sides are equal ($w = w$ and $l = l$).
A rectangle's diagonals are equal.

Squares

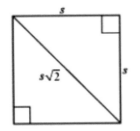

A square is a rectangle with four equal sides.
A diagonal of a square has length $s\sqrt{2}$, where s is the length of a side.

Quadrilaterals: Perimeter

- The perimeter of any quadrilateral is the sum of its four sides.

- Parallelograms and rectangles have opposite sides of equal length, so their perimeters are equal to twice the sum of two adjacent sides.

- Squares have four sides of equal length, so their perimeters are four times the length of one side.

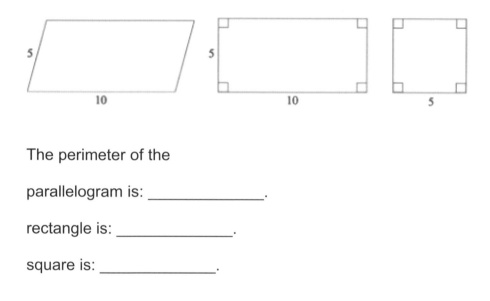

The perimeter of the

parallelogram is: _____.

rectangle is: _____.

square is: _____.

Quadrilaterals: Area

To find the area of a parallelogram, multiply its base by its height.

For a rectangle, multiply its length by its width.

For a square, just multiply a side length by itself.

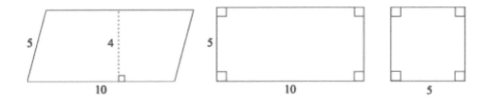

The area of the

parallelogram is: _____.

rectangle is: _____.

square is: _____.

Quadrilaterals: Practice Questions

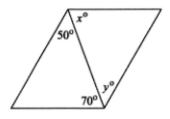

5. In the parallelogram above, what is the value of $x - y$?

(A) 10°
(B) 20°
(C) 40°
(D) 50°
(E) 60°

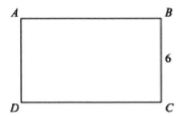

6. If $AB = AD + 4$, what is the area of rectangle $ABCD$?

(A) 6
(B) 10
(C) 24
(D) 32
(E) 60

7. A diagonal of a square has length $6\sqrt{2}$. What is the area of the square?

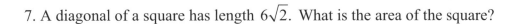

Summary

In this unit, you learned that:

- angles that share a line add up to 180°.

- when two lines intersect, the vertical (opposite) angles formed are equal to each other.

- just as there are always 360° in a circle, there are always 360° in angles around a point.

- when two parallel lines are cut by a transversal, small angles formed are all equal to one another, large angles formed are all equal to one another and small angles are supplementary to large angles.

- the angle measures of a triangle add up to 180°.

- the formula for the area of a triangle is $A = \dfrac{1}{2}bh$.

- the Pythagorean Theorem states that $a^2 + b^2 = c^2$, where a and b are the two shorter sides (or legs) of a right triangle and c is the longest side (or hypotenuse).

- any side of a triangle must be shorter than the sum of the other two sides and be longer than the difference of the other two sides.

- the angle measures of a quadrilateral add up to 360°.

- a parallelogram is a quadrilateral with two sets of parallel sides, opposite sides of equal length and opposite angles of equal measure.

- a rectangle is a parallelogram with four right angles and a square is a rectangle with four equal sides.

- the perimeter of any parallelogram can be found by adding its sides, and its area can be found by multiplying its base by its height (which are adjacent sides in a rectangle and a square).

Answer Key

1. D
2. C
3. 60
4. B
5. B
6. E
7. 36

Session 6: Sentence Completions Strategy

In this unit, you will learn how to:

- read the directions for Sentence Completions.

- identify the parts of the question and choices in Sentence Completions.

- distinguish between the different ways that Sentence Completions typically appear on the SAT.

- identify common sentence types in Sentence Completions.

- use keywords to steer you to the correct answer in Sentence Completions.

- apply Peterson's Technique for Sentence Completions to one- and two-blank sentences.

- eliminate wrong answers to improve your guessing on even the toughest Sentence Completions.

Note: Photocopying any part of this book is prohibited by law.

169

Sentence Completions: The Directions

These instructions will appear at the beginning of every Sentence Completions section.

Directions:

Each sentence below has one or two blanks, each blank indicating that something has been omitted. Beneath the sentence are five words or sets of words labeled A through E. Choose the word or set of words that, when inserted in the sentence, best fits the meaning of the sentence as a whole.

A discerning publishing agent can ------- promising material from a mass of submissions, separating the good from the bad.

(A) supplant
(B) dramatize
(C) finagle
(D) winnow
(E) overhaul

In your own words, what is your task in answering Sentence Completions?

_____

_____

Note: Photocopying any part of this book is prohibited by law.

170

What Are Sentence Completions?

A Sentence Completion is a sentence with a missing word or words. There will be one or two blanks, never more. Your job is to find the word or words that best complete the sentence.

Here's what a one-blank Sentence Completion question looks like:

1. Francisco was ------- about his first job interview, so he listened to his favorite CD to try to relax himself.

(A) pleased
(B) anxious
(C) confident
(D) delighted
(E) aggravated

Here's the same sentence as a two-blank Sentence Completion question.

2. Francisco was ------- about his first job interview, so he listened to his favorite CD to try to ------- himself.

(A) pleased . . calm
(B) anxious . . compose
(C) nervous . . agitate
(D) delighted . . perturb
(E) worried . . demoralize

What makes two-blank sentences harder?

_____

_____

What makes them easier?

_____

_____

Note: Photocopying any part of this book is prohibited by law.

171

Sentence Completions: The Facts

There are about 19 Sentence Completions on the SAT. Here are the basic facts about them.

Where They Are

Sentence Completion questions are:

- in the Critical Reading sections of the test.

- arranged from easier to harder. (The first Sentence Completions in a section are easier than the last ones.)

What They Test

Sentence Completions test your:

- ability to read and understand a sentence.

- powers of logic.

- vocabulary.

How They Test

Sentence Completions set up relationships, such as definitions and contrasts, to test your ability to follow the path of a sentence and fill in the missing pieces.

Note: Photocopying any part of this book is prohibited by law.

172

What You Won't See

You will never see a Sentence Completion that looks like this...

The magician's hat was -------.

(A) green
(B) blue
(C) red
(D) yellow
(E) brown

Why won't you see any Sentence Completions that look like this one?

_____

_____

_____

Common Sentence Structures

Many Sentence Completions fall into a few predictable categories.

Green Light

Green Light sentences continue one thought from beginning to end:

- Definition sentences: Define one of the words in the sentence.

- Cause-and-effect sentences: Describe an effect and its cause.

U-Turn

U-Turn sentences include:

- Contrast sentences: A situation is set up in the sentence and then contradicted by some other information.

- Comparison sentences: Two things are compared to one another.

S-Curve

S-Curve sentences can be difficult. They include:

- Flow sentences: Are long, often with hard vocabulary.

- Logic sentences: Can be hard to follow because their logic is complicated. For example, they may combine a Green Light and a U-Turn sentence.

Keywords in Sentence Completions

Keywords help you figure out what type of sentence you are dealing with.

Sentence Type	Common Keywords
Green Light	and, because, thus, so, as well, hence, since, semicolon
U-Turn	however, but, yet, not, far from being, despite, although
S-Curve	can contain keywords from either of the other two sentence types

Your Turn

Choose the correct sentence type for each sentence below.

3. When opponents of the proposed legislation speak of it, they are not ------- of his motives; indeed, they support the end to which he aspires, but they differ in their opinions concerning the ------- of the suggested means.

_____ Green Light _____ U-Turn _____ S-Curve

4. Postage stamps are often used to ------- important people; for example, a colorful new bird stamp was recently launched to celebrate John James Audubon.

_____ Green Light _____ U-Turn _____ S-Curve

5. The wedding was praised as a ------- and ------- event, despite the fact that temperatures soared and the venue lacked air conditioning.

_____ Green Light _____ U-Turn _____ S-Curve

Peterson's Technique for Sentence Completions

Here is Peterson's Technique for Sentence Completions, which you should use on every Sentence Completions question.

Step 1: Read the Sentence

Make as much sense of it as you can. Don't look at the answer choices yet.

Step 2: Predict the Answer

Try to predict what the correct answer will be (without looking at the answer choices).

Step 3: Find the Choice that Best Matches Your Prediction

If you're not sure, cross out the choices that sound wrong and focus on those that remain. Even if you can't narrow it down to one choice, you can greatly improve your chances of guessing correctly.

Step 4: Read the Sentence with Your Choice Inserted

Sometimes a choice might feel right by itself, but when you read the completed sentence, you realize that it doesn't actually make sense. If a choice sounds wrong, it probably is.

Note: Photocopying any part of this book is prohibited by law.

176

Applying Peterson's Technique for Sentence Completions

6. One could only describe the counselor's behavior as -------; she always kept her own emotions out of the situation.

(A) indulgent
(B) objective
(C) callous
(D) generous
(E) irrational

Step 1: Read the sentence

If you need to, cover the answer choices so you don't read them. What is the sentence saying?

_____

Step 2: Predict the Answer

We know that the counselor is described a certain way and that she keeps her emotions out of things. The missing word will be the one that describes her behavior, and it will mean something like "keeping her emotions out of the way."

Prediction: _____

Step 3: Find the Choice that Best Matches Your Prediction

Which choice best matches your prediction?

_____

Step 4: Read the Sentence with Your Choice Inserted

Read the sentence to yourself. How does it sound with your choice inserted?

_____

Peterson's Technique for Two-Blank Sentences

On the SAT, you will see some Sentence Completions that have two blanks rather than just one. How does the technique work for these sentences?

Step 1: Read the Sentence

- Read the sentence and make as much sense of it as you can.

- Two blanks may make the sentence harder to understand, but try to get a sense of what the sentence is saying and which blank is easier to fill.

Step 2: Predict the Easier Blank

- Make a prediction for the easier blank, whichever one that is for you.

- Don't be afraid to try the second blank first. It's often easier to handle.

Step 3: Narrow the Choices

- Focus only on the choices for the easier blank.

- Cross out the choices that don't work.

Step 4: Fill In Choices

- Read each of the remaining choices back into the sentence.

- Focus on the other blank. Eliminate the choices that don't work for it.

Step 5: Make Your Final Choice

- Pick the choice that works for both blanks.

- Read the entire sentence again, verifying that the answer works for both blanks.

Note: Photocopying any part of this book is prohibited by law.

178

Applying Peterson's Technique for Two-Blank Sentences

7. During the Great Depression, many farm families ------- across the Plains in search of a better life and more ------- land.

(A) wandered .. arid
(B) visited .. barren
(C) sped .. dusty
(D) vacationed .. healthy
(E) migrated .. fertile

Step 1: Read the Sentence

Read the sentence to yourself, avoiding looking at the answer choices. What is the sentence saying?

_____

Step 2: Predict the Easier Blank

Which blank seems to be easier? _____

What keywords can you find? _____

Prediction for the easier blank: _____

Step 3: Narrow the Choices

Which choices can you eliminate for the second blank? _____

Step 4: Fill in Choices

Read the remaining choices back into the sentence, eliminating choices that don't work for the first blank.

What choices can you eliminate for the first blank? _____

Step 5: Make Your Final Choice

What choice works for both blanks? _____

Read the sentence back to yourself. Does it make sense? _____

Note: Photocopying any part of this book is prohibited by law.

179

Difficult Sentence Completions

On the SAT, you will see some tough Sentence Completions. So what makes these questions so hard?

Vocabulary

Complex vocabulary may appear in the sentence or in the answer choices, but usually not in both.

> 8. The thief was an accomplished prevaricator; one could hardly tell if anything he said was mendacious or -------.

"Prevaricator" probably means: _____

"Mendacious" probably means: _____

Prediction for the blank: _____

Long or Confusing Sentences

Long or confusing sentences have hard-to-follow logic (S-Curve sentences).

> 9. In contrast to her more ------- colleagues, the chemist was known for breakthroughs that derived not from hours at the lab, but rather from days at the beach or long walks in the woods, a situation that generated significant resentment from her diligent peers.

This sentence has several contrasts that can throw you off track. The key is to reduce it to the basics.

What this sentence basically means:

_____

_____

Prediction for the blank: _____

Note: Photocopying any part of this book is prohibited by law.

180

Eliminating Wrong Direction Choices

If you can identify the sentence type, you can often tell whether you need a positive or a negative word for the blank. In the example below, we've hidden the answer choices.

10. Despite the many positive reviews of the restaurant, the food was actually -------.

  (A) -------
  (B) -------
  (C) -------
  (D) -------
  (E) -------

What kind of sentence is this?

_____

What kind of word do you need for the blank?

_____

Eliminating Choices in Two-Blank Sentences

Even if you are stumped on one blank of a two-blank sentence, you can work with the other blank to narrow your options.

> 11. Palm trees, while ------- in tropical climates, are rarely found in climates that have ------- winters.
>
> (A) common . . mild
> (B) unusual . . harsh
> (C) troubling . . enduring
> (D) pleasant . . short
> (E) typical . . severe

If you were running short on time and only had time to look at the first blank, what could you do?

Make a prediction for the first blank: _____

Which choices can you eliminate based on your prediction for the first blank?

_____

_____

Practice Questions

12. Sometimes considered ------- and outdated, the abacus continues to be used as a calculation device in many cultures.

(A) timeless
(B) antiquated
(C) historic
(D) indispensable
(E) premature

13. While the original design for the building featured many surprising and ------- elements, the final version was quite -------.

(A) interesting .. believable
(B) unconventional .. traditional
(C) unexpected .. shocking
(D) challenging .. bewildering
(E) harmonic .. jarring

14. A discerning publishing agent can ------- promising material from a mass of submissions, separating the good from the bad.

(A) supplant
(B) dramatize
(C) finagle
(D) winnow
(E) overhaul

15. Novice rafters tend to ------- the danger posed by the river because of its ------- appearance, even though warning signs are posted around the area.

(A) underestimate .. placid
(B) perceive .. restrained
(C) exaggerate .. deceptive
(D) belittle .. rugged
(E) disregard .. ominous

Summary

In this unit, you learned that:

- Sentence Completions test your reading, logic, and vocabulary.

- Sentence Completions are sentences with one or two missing words, never more.

- Sentence Completions can be Green Light, U-Turn, or S- Curve sentences.

- looking for clues in keywords will help you make better predictions.

- Peterson's Technique for Sentence Completions will help you answer Sentence Completions more quickly and more accurately.

- on two-blank sentences, you should start with the easier blank.

- difficult Sentence Completions contain tough vocabulary or tough sentence structure.

- if you're stuck, you may be able to eliminate some choices and guess.

Answer Key

1. B
2. B
6. B
7. E
11. E
12. B
13. B
14. D
15. A

Note: Photocopying any part of this book is prohibited by law.

184

Session 7: Algebra Fundamentals

In this unit, you will learn to:

- combine like terms.

- evaluate expressions.

- simplify algebraic expressions.

- solve linear equations.

- solve equations with two variables.

- solve inequalities.

- factor expressions.

- perform operations with exponents and radicals.

Combining Terms

A term is:

- a **number** (such as 2 or 4.99 or $\frac{2}{3}$ or $\sqrt{20}$)

- a **variable** (such as x or k)

- a **number coefficient and a variable together** (such as $5x$ or $6\sqrt{k}$)

Terms make up expressions (such as $5x + 3$) and equations (such as $5x + 3 = 23$). On the SAT you'll need to combine terms to make them easier to handle. But only *like* terms can be combined.

Like Terms

Terms are alike when they have the exact same variable (including the power of that variable).

Which of the terms below can be combined?

x	y	xy	$3x^2y$	x^2y^2
x^2y	3.5	xy^2	-3	$2x$
$3y$	1	$-2y$	$3.5x$	$3xy$

Exercise

Simplify the following expressions by combining like terms.

$x + 3x =$ _____

$2a + 3b + 4a =$ _____

$5x + 4y =$ _____

$3a + 2ab + 2b + 6b + 7ab =$ _____

Combining Like Terms: Practice Questions

1. Which of the following is equal to the expression $2x + 2y + 3x$?

(A) $4x + 3y$
(B) $7xy$
(C) $2y + x$
(D) $5x + 2y$
(E) $3x$

2. $18a + 8ab + b^2 - a$ can be rewritten as which of the following?

(A) $17a + 8ab + b^2$
(B) $19a + 8ab + b^2$
(C) $17ab^2 + 8ab$
(D) $26ab^2$
(E) $10ab + b^2$

Evaluating Algebraic Expressions

To evaluate an algebraic expression:

1. Plug in the given value for the variable.
2. Work through the computation, following the order of operations.

Example

What is the value of $3(x-2)-2x$?

Exercise

What is the value of $x^2 + 7x$ if . . .

$x = 2$? _____

$x = 3$? _____

$x = -2$? _____

Evaluating Algebraic Expressions: Practice Questions

3. When $x = -3$, what is the value of $2x - 2(3-x)$?

(A) -18
(B) -15
(C) -9
(D) -6
(E) -3

4. If $x = 5$, what is the value of $3x + 2(x - 10)$?

(A) 0
(B) 5
(C) 15
(D) 25
(E) 35

Solving Equations – Single Step Solutions

When you solve an equation, you find the value of a variable.

You solve by getting the variable all by itself on one side of the equals sign. This process is called isolating the variable.

Example

Look at the following equation:
$$x + 2 = 7$$

Step 1: Determine what is happening to the variable.

Step 2: Determine what you need to do to get the variable, *x*, by itself.

Step 3: Perform this operation with the same number on both sides of the equation.

Exercise:

If $3y = 12,$ what is the value of y?

Solving Equations – Multi-Step Solutions

Sometimes, there is more than one operation that has been done to the variable. In such cases, you need to "undo" what's been done to the variable in a particular order:

1. Undo any additions or subtractions.
2. Undo any divisions.
3. Undo any multiplications.

Example

Look at the following equation:

$$2x + 7 = 15$$

Step 1: Determine which operations are being done to the variable.

Step 2: Undo any additions or subtractions.

Step 3: Undo any divisions.

Step 4: Undo any multiplications.

Practice Question

5. If $4x + 3 = 19$, then what is the value of x?

(A) 4
(B) 5.5
(C) 11
(D) 16
(E) 22

Note: Photocopying any part of this book is prohibited by law.

190

Solving Equations Requiring Simplification

Sometimes, you need to simplify one or both sides of an equation before you can "undo" what's been done to the variable. In such cases, solving equations is a three-step process:

Look at the following equation:

$$3(x-2)-2x=8$$

Step 1: Simplify the expressions in the equation by using PEMDAS

Step 2: Combine like terms.

Step 3: Solve by isolating the variable.

Practice Question

6. If $2(x+3)=13,$ then what is the value of x?

(A) 2
(B) 2.5
(C) 3
(D) 3.5
(E) 7

Solving for an Expression Containing Both *x* and *y*

Sometimes, a question will ask you to solve for an expression such as *x* + *y* or *x* − *y*.

For these questions, you can solve for the expression directly; that is, you do not need to solve for *x* and *y* individually.

Example

7. If $2x + 3y = 13$ and $3x + 2y = 32$, then what is the value of $x + y$?

    (A) 4
    (B) 6
    (C) 9
    (D) 15
    (E) 45

Do you see the shortcut?

Always read the question carefully. What's different about this example?

8. If $2x + 3y = 13$ and $3x + 2y = 32$, then what is the value of $3x + 3y$?

Here's a tougher example:

9. If $10x + 3y = 23$ and $8x + 5y = 21$, then what is the value of $x - y$?

Solving for x in Terms of y

Sometimes, a question will ask you to solve for one variable in terms of another. For these questions, isolate the variable you're asked for by undoing what is being done to it. The only difference will be that the other variable will appear in your answer.

Example

If $5x + 3y = 2$, what is the value of y in terms of x?

Step 1: Determine which operations are being done to the variable.

Step 2: Undo any additions or subtractions.

Step 3: Undo any divisions.

Step 4: Undo any multiplications.

10. If $3x + 2y = 7$, what is the value of x?

(A) $7 + 3y$

(B) $\dfrac{3 + 7y}{2}$

(C) $\dfrac{3 - 2y}{7}$

(D) $2y - 7$

(E) $\dfrac{7 - 2y}{3}$

You can also solve problems such as these by plugging in numbers. In the question above, you can pick a value for y and then figure out what x would be.

Solving Inequalities

< means _____

> means _____

≤ means _____

≥ means _____

Inequalities are solved just like standard equations are solved. The differences are:

- the answer is a set of values rather than just a single number.

- when you multiply or divide by a negative number, you must flip the direction of the inequality sign.

Examples

$3x - 6 > 18$

$-5x + 7 \le 22$

Solving Inequalities: Practice Questions

11. If $2x + 12 \geq 4$, which of the following must be true?

(A) $x < 2$
(B) $x \geq -4$
(C) $x = -4$
(D) $x \leq 4$
(E) $x > -2$

12. Which of the following exactly identifies the values of x that satisfy $-4x + 2 < 18$?

(A) $x > -16$
(B) $x > 4$
(C) $x < 4$
(D) $x > -4$
(E) $x < -4$

Factoring

Factoring consists of two steps:

1. Remove the greatest common factor from each term by dividing through by it.
2. List the factors side by side.

Examples

How could you simplify the expression below?

$4x - 4z$

Here's another example: $8xyz - 4yb$

Factor out the number first: _____

Then factor out the variables: _____

Exercises

Practice factoring the following expressions:

$3x + 3y =$ _____

$3mn - 9n =$ _____

$15y + 60xy =$ _____

$6z - yz^2 =$ _____

$4x + x =$ _____

Factoring: Practice Question

13. Which of the following is the result when the expression $14axz + 42bz$ is fully factored?

(A) $7(2axz + 6bz)$
(B) $7a(2xz + 6bz)$
(C) $7z(2ax + 6b)$
(D) $14(axz + 3bz)$
(E) $14z(ax + 3b)$

Note: Photocopying any part of this book is prohibited by law.

197

Exponents

Exponents are a form of shorthand. What do the following expressions mean? Simplify each expression.

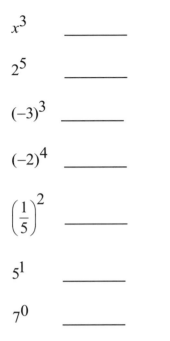

x^3 _____

2^5 _____

$(-3)^3$ _____

$(-2)^4$ _____

$\left(\dfrac{1}{5}\right)^2$ _____

5^1 _____

7^0 _____

Adding and Subtracting Terms Containing Exponents

Remember that only like terms can be combined.

Just add or subtract the coefficients and carry the like bases with their exponent along.

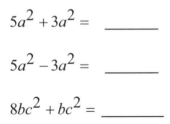

$5a^2 + 3a^2 =$ _____

$5a^2 - 3a^2 =$ _____

$8bc^2 + bc^2 =$ _____

Multiplying Terms Containing Exponents

To multiply terms with powers that have the same base, keep the base and add the exponents.

Examples

$$3^5 \times 3^2 = 3^{5+2} = 3^7$$
$$g^2 \times g^3 = g^{2+3} = g^5$$

Exercises

$$c^4 \times c^5 \times c = c^{5+4+1} = \underline{\hspace{2cm}}$$

$$7a^2 \times 8a^3 = (7 \times 8)(a^{2+3}) = \underline{\hspace{2cm}}$$

$$(4x^2 y)(-3xyz) = (4)(-3)(x^{2+1})(y^{1+1})(z) = \underline{\hspace{2cm}}$$

$$(6abc^2)(5bc^3) = \underline{\hspace{2cm}}$$

Dividing Terms Containing Exponents

To divide powers with the same base, keep the base and subtract the exponents.

Examples

$$3^5 \div 3^2 = 3^5 - 3^2 = 3^3$$

$$\frac{r^7}{r^3} = r^4$$

Exercises

$$\frac{12s^4 t^6 u}{4s^3 tu} = (12 \div 4)(s^{4-3})(t^{6-1})(u^{1-1}) = \underline{\hspace{3cm}}$$

$$\frac{10q^2 rs^6}{2r^3} = \underline{\hspace{3cm}}$$

Raising a Power to a Power

To raise a power to a power, keep the base and multiply the exponents. Where there is a coefficient, raise the coefficient to the power.

Examples

$(3^5)^2 = 3^{5 \times 2} = 3^{10}$

$(7xy^3)^2 = (7^2)(x^{1 \times 2})(y^{3 \times 2}) = 49x^2y^6$

Practice Questions

14. $(x^8)(x^5)$ is equivalent to which of the following?

(A) x^{40}
(B) x^{13}
(C) x^3
(D) $8x^5$
(E) $40x$

15. Which of the following is equivalent to $\dfrac{a^6 \times a^4}{a^2}$?

(A) a^5
(B) a^8
(C) a^{12}
(D) a^{22}
(E) a^{24}

Square Roots and Radicals

Taking the square root of a number is the opposite of squaring a number. The square root of a number is the number that, when multiplied by itself, equals the original number.

The symbol $\sqrt{}$ is called the square root or radical sign. It indicates that you should take the square root of the number beneath it.

Example

$\sqrt{9} = 3$ because $3 \times 3 = 9$.

What is the square root of:

16?   36?   81?   100?   10,000? x^2? x^4?

Perfect Squares

- A perfect square is a number whose square root is an integer.

- 4 is a perfect square because $\sqrt{4}$ equals 2.

- Some numbers do not have integer square roots.

Which of the following are perfect squares?

3   4   6   8   9   12   16   20   25

Simplifying Radicals

When the number under the radical sign is not a perfect square, you can simplify the radical by taking the square roots of its factors.

Example

Step 1: Determine whether the number under the radical sign has any factors that are perfect squares.

Can $\sqrt{22}$ be simplified?

Can $\sqrt{28}$ be simplified?

Step 2: Write the number under the radical sign as the product of the perfect square and another factor.

The number 28 has a perfect square factor of 4.

Step 3: Continue simplifying until the number under the radical sign has no perfect square factors.

Note: Photocopying any part of this book is prohibited by law.

202

Square Roots and Variables

Sometimes, you will be asked to take the square root of expressions containing variables.

Example

Step 1: Determine whether the variable under the radical sign has any factors that are perfect squares.

Can $\sqrt{y}$ be simplified?

Can $\sqrt{y^5}$ be simplified?

Step 2: Write the variable term under the radical sign as the product of the perfect square and another factor.

$$\sqrt{y^5} =$$

Step 3: Evaluate the perfect square. Continue simplifying until the number under the radical sign has no perfect square factors.

Exercise

Simplify the following expressions:

$\sqrt{16x^4 y^3 z} =$ _____

$\sqrt{75a^5 y^4 z} =$ _____

Note: Photocopying any part of this book is prohibited by law.

203

Adding and Subtracting Radicals:

Rule 1: You can only add or subtract roots that have the same number under the radical sign.

Rule 2: Work with radicals in the same way you would work with variables: add or subtract the number coefficients outside the radical sign and carry the radical along.

Example

In the same way that $3a + a = 3a + 1a = 4a$:

$$3\sqrt{7} + \sqrt{7} = 3\sqrt{7} + 1\sqrt{7} = 4\sqrt{7}.$$

In the same way that $3a - a = 3a - 1a = 2a$:

$$3\sqrt{7} - \sqrt{7} = 3\sqrt{7} - 1\sqrt{7} = 2\sqrt{7}.$$

Exercise

$2\sqrt{x} - \sqrt{x} + 6\sqrt{x} = \underline{\hspace{2cm}}$

Multiplying Radicals

To multiply roots, multiply the values under the radicals, and then simplify if necessary.

Example

$$\sqrt{2} \times \sqrt{12} = \sqrt{2 \times 12} = \sqrt{24}$$

Since 24 has a perfect square factor of 4, it can be simplified:

$$\sqrt{24} = \sqrt{4 \times 6} = \sqrt{4} \times \sqrt{6} = 2\sqrt{6}.$$

If the radicals have coefficients, multiply the coefficients and the radical parts separately. Again, simplify if necessary.

Example

$$3\sqrt{2} \times 5\sqrt{12} = (3 \times 5)(\sqrt{2} \times \sqrt{12})$$
$$= 15\sqrt{24}$$
$$= 15 \times 2\sqrt{6}$$
$$= 30\sqrt{6}$$

Exercises

$5\sqrt{6} \times 4\sqrt{8} =$ _____

$7\sqrt{2} \times 5\sqrt{8} =$ _____

Dividing Radicals

To divide roots, divide the values under the radicals, and then simplify.

Example

$$\frac{\sqrt{18}}{\sqrt{6}} = \sqrt{\frac{18}{6}} = \sqrt{\frac{3}{1}} = \sqrt{3}$$

If the radicals have coefficients, divide the coefficients and the radical parts separately.

Example

$$\frac{12\sqrt{48}}{3\sqrt{6}} = \frac{12}{3} \times \sqrt{\frac{48}{6}}$$
$$= 4\sqrt{8}$$
$$= 4 \times \sqrt{4 \times 2}$$
$$= 4 \times 2\sqrt{2}$$
$$= 8\sqrt{2}$$

Exercise

$$\frac{16\sqrt{20}}{2\sqrt{5}} = \underline{\hspace{3cm}}$$

Note: Photocopying any part of this book is prohibited by law.

206

Practice Questions

16. Which of the following is equivalent to $(\sqrt{5a})(5\sqrt{a})$?

(A) $5a$
(B) $5a^2$
(C) $25a$
(D) $5a\sqrt{5}$
(E) $\sqrt{5a}$

17. $\dfrac{30x\sqrt{20x^2}}{2x\sqrt{5x^2}} =$

(A) 15
(B) $15x$
(C) 30
(D) 60
(E) $60x$

Summary

In this unit, you learned that:

- only like terms can be combined.

- you evaluate an algebraic expression by plugging in the value for the variable and doing the computation according to the order of operations.
- to solve an equation, isolate the variable by "undoing" what was done to it.

- to solve an equation requiring multiple steps, first undo any additions or subtractions, followed by any divisions and then any multiplications.

- inequalities are solved in the same way as equalities are solved, with two major differences: answers are a set of values and the inequality symbol must be reversed when multiplying or dividing by a negative value.

- terms with the same base (including the exponent) can be combined by adding or subtracting the coefficients and carrying the like bases and their exponent.

- to multiply terms with powers that have the same base, keep the base and add the exponents.

- to divide powers with the same base, keep the base and subtract the exponents.

- to raise a power to a power, keep the base and multiply the exponents.

- radicals are simplified by taking the square root of any perfect square factors of the value under the radical sign.

- add or subtract roots by adding/subtracting the number coefficients outside the radical sign and carrying the radical along.

- multiply or divide roots by multiplying/dividing the coefficients and the radical parts separately.

Answer Key

1. D
2. A
3. A
4. B
5. A
6. D
7. C
8. 27
9. 1
10. E
11. B
12. D
13. E
14. B
15. B
16. D
17. C

Note: Photocopying any part of this book is prohibited by law.

210

Session 7: Essay Writing: You Be the Judge

In this unit, you will learn to:

- think like a scorer.

- identify what qualities earn essays different scores.

- judge student essays for yourself using the SAT's Scoring Guide.

- earn a 4 or higher on your essay.

Note: Photocopying any part of this book is prohibited by law.

211

SAT Essay Facts

As part of the Writing section, you will be asked to write a short essay. A prompt will present one or two quotes about an issue and then direct you to write an essay that takes and supports a position on that issue.

Your essay score determines about _____ 1/3 _____ of your points for the Writing section. That means your essay score makes up a little more than 10 percent of your total score on the SAT.

How Your Essay Is Scored

Two trained readers will each give your essay a score from 1 to 6, so your total score can range from 2 to 12.

If you don't write on the assigned topic, no matter how brilliant your ideas are, you'll receive a zero from both scorers.

Timing

You'll have 25 minutes to read the prompt, brainstorm your ideas, plan and write your essay, and proofread. This may sound like a lot to accomplish, but the essay scorers know the time limitation, so they're not expecting a perfect essay. Instead, they're expecting a quality first draft.

Your Turn

1. What makes a good first draft? What kinds of errors might be acceptable, and what kinds of errors will hurt your score?

explain what is ok, stick with the topic. What can
hurt you? spelling, incomplete sentense, getting off
topic.

Note: Photocopying any part of this book is prohibited by law.

212

Think Like a Scorer

In this SAT course, you'll learn how to have the right attitude and use the right method when you write your essay. Those two factors will help you write the best essay you can. To truly succeed, though, you need the primary key to writing a successful essay: knowing what your audience wants.

The rest of this unit is about understanding how SAT essays are scored. If you know what the essay scorers want, how they think, and what they consider a highly effective essay, you will know what it takes to impress them and get the score you want and deserve.

Your Turn

Use the statements below about scorers to determine how you can make your essay stand out.

2. Scorers spend about a minute reading each essay. This means:

    Get to the point

3. Scorers read hundreds to thousands of essays on the same topic. This means:

    Be creative

4. The essay is the only part of your SAT not scored by computer. This means:

    Try your best

5. Scorers are current or former teachers. This means:

    They know when you bullshit.

Note: Photocopying any part of this book is prohibited by law.

213

The Scoring Guide

This table lists the five writing elements that each reader evaluates.

Element	This includes
Development and Support	<ul><li>how fully the essay responds to the prompt</li><li>the essay's sense of completeness</li><li>the essay's focus on the issue and avoidance of "filler"</li><li>the quality and sufficiency of examples supporting the writer's position</li><li>the depth of critical thinking and reasoning</li></ul>
Organization	<ul><li>the order of sentences and paragraphs</li><li>the use of effective transitions</li><li>the flow of ideas from the essay's introduction to its body through to its conclusion</li></ul>
Language	<ul><li>how accurately words and phrases communicate the author's ideas</li><li>how well the author varies word choice</li><li>the level of vocabulary the author displays</li></ul>
Sentence Structure	<ul><li>how well the author uses a variety of sentence types that are correctly punctuated</li><li>how well and often the author varies sentence structure in meaningful and purposeful ways</li></ul>
Conventions	<ul><li>how correctly the author uses punctuation (commas, apostrophes, periods, colons, etc.)</li><li>the author's correctness in grammar and mechanics (subject/ verb agreement, verb tense, subject/pronoun agreement, etc.)</li></ul>

Overall Score

The essay is scored holistically—which means that the final score is based on an overall impression. Essay readers won't keep track of errors or assign a subscore for each writing element to determine a final score.

The best plan is to make your essay as good as possible according to all five scoring elements. Identify and improve your writing weaknesses but also take advantage of your writing strengths.

Note: Photocopying any part of this book is prohibited by law.

214

What the Scores Mean

How do the readers give your essay a score from 1 to 6?

Score	What It Means
6	• The essay fully develops a point of view on the issue, showing high-level critical thinking and using appropriate and ample evidence. • Its organization and focus are apparent throughout. • It demonstrates a skillful use of language and sentence structure. • It is free or mostly free of errors.
5	• The essay develops a point of view on the issue, showing critical thinking and generally using appropriate and ample evidence. • It demonstrates organization and focus. • It contains appropriately varied language and sentence structure. • It is generally free of errors.
4	• The essay develops a point of view on the issue, showing some critical thinking and generally using adequate evidence. • It is somewhat focused and has a somewhat organized progression of ideas. • It inconsistently uses varied language and sentence structure. • It has some errors.
3	• The essay develops a point of view on the issue, showing some critical thinking but presenting inadequate evidence. • It is limited in its organization, with some flaws in the progression of ideas. • It demonstrates some weaknesses or errors in vocabulary and sentence structure. • It has several errors.
2	• The essay only partially develops a point of view on the issue, showing weak critical thinking and using inadequate evidence. • It is poorly organized. • It demonstrates a limited vocabulary and errors in sentence structure. • It has serious errors that confuse meaning.
1	• The essay fails to develop a point of view on the issue or use appropriate evidence. • It is unorganized. • It demonstrates multiple errors in word choice and sentence structure. • It has serious errors that interfere with meaning.

4 versus 3

Compare the descriptions of essays that earn a 4 and essays that earn a 3.

Essays that earn a 3:	Essays that earn a 4:
do not completely answer the question given in the writing assignment.	answer the question given in the writing assignment.
use inconsistent logic or inadequate examples.	use logic and relevant examples.
have limited organization.	are organized.
use little or no variety in sentence structure and word choice.	use at least some variety in sentence structure and word choice.
have errors in sentence structure, word choice, grammar, and mechanics.	have few or no significant errors in sentence structure, word choice, grammar, and mechanics.

Get Ready to Score

Here's a prompt like the one you'll see on the SAT. Think about how you would compose an essay based on this prompt.

Directions: Think carefully about the issue presented in the quote below and the assignment that follows it.

To be nobody-but-yourself—in a world which is doing its best, night and day, to make you everybody else—means to fight the hardest battle which any human being can fight; and never stop fighting.
e.e. cummings

Assignment: What is your view on the idea that it is more important to be true to yourself than to do what others expect you to do? Plan and write an essay developing your point of view, supporting it with reasoning and examples taken from your reading, studies, experience, or observations.

After you've looked over the prompt, it's your turn to be the judge. You'll see several student essays based on this prompt. Read each carefully and decide what scores they deserve.

When judging the essays, remember the five elements of the Scoring Guide. Fill them in now so you remember them:

* *Organization* _____

* *Language* _____

* *Sentence Structure* _____

_____

_____

Note: Photocopying any part of this book is prohibited by law.

217

Student Essay #1

You should be true to yourself rather than conforming to the expectations that others have of you. This is true. Sometimes its easier just to go along with the crowd, and sometimes other people mean well when they tell you to do something, but they don't know you as well as you do, so its important to listen to your inner consciounce.

I know this first hand. In my highschool there is alot of pressure to be this way or that way. When I was in Marching Band alot of other musicians would smoke cigarettes before we played and they were considered the cool group, so at first I thought that if I smoked cigarette than I would be more accepted by them. But I didn't like the way the cigarette tasted so I said no after that. At first I was given the cold shoulder for being "straight", but after that the other musicians came to see that I was just being true to myself. In time they came to respect me for who I am.

Sometimes its good to listen to the advice that others want to give you because they mean well and sometimes they have good ideas. Even if you make mistakes they will be your own mistakes and you can learn from them and grow wiser.

If you just try do what everyone expects of you you'll never figure out what it is you are best at and really enjoy doing. Like the wise man once said, "To thine own self be true."

Score (1-6): _2 (5)_

Reasons: _Sentence Structure, needs more examples, confusing grammar. Final thought._

Student Essay #2

It's important to be true to yourself and not conform to do what others expect you to do. An example of this is the decision of what to do after high school.

In my high school, more students want to go to college after leaving, which is a decision I made because it is harder to get a job without a college degree and you can learn what you want to do for a living by taking college courses. Others want to join the military. Which also make sense for them, since they can learn career skills while at the same time they serving their country. Another example of the importance of true to yourself is in politics. In tough times people like to rally around the flag and supported the president. This shows the world that we are one nation united together. But we are given the right to vote. The majority rule, and if the majority decide that the government is doing a good job, they will vote him back into office next time. But it's important to be true to yourself when entering the ballot box and pick the man (or woman) who you thinks best for the job.

There are lots of ocassions when you have to decide whats right for yourself, even though lots of people will think something else. It can sometimes be hard to be true to yourself, but this is a free country and that's what you are supposed to do.

Score (1-6): _2_

Reasons: _? I thought it was about his high school decision because that's his/her topic sentence. Too much "filler", but ungood examples?_

Student Essay #3

We all face pressures to meet the expectations that others have for us. Sometimes these expectations are based on sound reasons, such as the expectations that your parents have for you to try to do your best in school. Other times, however, the expectations that others have may be based on misguided assumptions, unquestioned traditions, or outright prejudice. For these reasons it's important to be true to yourself, to be "nobody-but-yourself," and be willing to take a stand for who you are and what you believe in.

I have experienced both positive and negative expectations based on prejudice. As a Korean American, I know that others generally expect me to be a straight-A student, and it doesn't bother me a lot that I happen to fit these expectations of the "model immigrant" stereotype. But others in my school haven't been so fortunate. My school has a small minority of students who are from Pakistan. They used to be treated about as well as any other minority.

However, the atmosphere is quite different now. Now all of a sudden it became very important to some of my classmates that the Pakistanis in my school were Muslim. Some of my more thick-headed classmates viewed them as the enemy, and called them names and even threatened them. I could tell that several of my Pakistani classmates were becoming afraid.

I'm ashamed to admit that although I was upset by what was going on, at first I did little to stop it. It's frankly a lot easier to keep your head low. And besides, I've never been terribly keen on confronting class bullies. But one day I saw my friend Samir, or Sam, as he prefers to be called, being threatened by two such bullies. For reasons that weren't really clear to me then I came to Sam's defense, and to our surprise, the bullies backed down.

What I finally came to realize is that I did not stick up for Sam simply out of friendship, although that should have been reason enough. I finally saw that I had to be true to my convictions, or else I wouldn't be much better than the bullies. I am glad that I did what I did, and I am hopeful that in the future I will always be willing to stand up to my convictions and resist the temptation to conform to the wishes of the crowd.

Score (1-6): _5_

Reasons: _Nice?!_

Note: Photocopying any part of this book is prohibited by law.

220

How to Get a 4 or Higher

Now that you've seen several essays, you probably have a better sense of what it takes to get a high score. Your essay must take a stand on the issue in the prompt, defend its points with examples, be well organized, use correct English with few errors in grammar and punctuation, and be easy to read.

Your Turn

Identify each statement below as true or false.

6. _____ Don't waste time planning your ideas. Time is short, so you should start writing as soon as you've read the prompt.

7. _____ You shouldn't include ideas that are unrelated to the topic of your essay, no matter how interesting those ideas are.

8. _____ You lose points for spelling errors.

9. _____ There's no need to proofread your essay.

Summary

In this unit, you learned that:

- readers evaluate an essay's development and support, organization, language, sentence structure, and conventions.

- essays are scored holistically—which means that the final score is based on an overall impression, rather than a strict formula.

- two readers will score your essay from 1 to 6 for a combined score of 2 to 12.

- by understanding the scoring formula and planning your time, you can get a 4 or higher on your own essay.

Session 7: SAT Grammar II

In this unit, you will learn to:

- master common grammar concepts tested on the SAT.

- recognize common SAT grammar mistakes.

- solve typical SAT grammar questions.

Comparisons

Comparing Two of a Kind

When a sentence includes a comparison, the parts of the sentence involved in the comparison must match. What's wrong with the following sentence? How can it be corrected?

> Like an orange, you can get juice from a grapefruit.

Whenever you see a comparison in the SAT writing section, check the two parts of the sentence to make sure the author of the sentence compares like things.

Comparison Words

How do you know when to use "like" or "as"? Use the following rules:

- When the phrases being compared both contain a verb, you must use "as."
- If one of the phrases does not contain a verb, then you must use "like."

Is the following sentence grammatically correct?

> She sings beautifully, just like her mother did.

Comparisons Exercise

Rewrite each of the following sentences using a correct comparison.

Like her sister, math is Lela's favorite subject.

Unlike the original statue, plastic was used to make the copy.

Like tomatoes, you can make sauce from peppers.

His opinion was different from his brother.

Note: Photocopying any part of this book is prohibited by law.

225

Adjectives and Adverbs

- Adjectives and adverbs are description words.
- Adjectives describe nouns (things).
- Adverbs describe verbs (actions).

The tall, green grass rustled in the breeze.

Which words are adjectives? Which word is an adverb?

Making Comparisons

Adjectives and adverbs don't just describe nouns and verbs. They can also compare them. To compare two things, add "–er" to an adjective. Use an adjective to complete this sentence:

The chair is _____ than the table.

You can also add more or less before an adjective or adverb. Use an adverb to complete this sentence:

She sang more _____ than she ever had before.

To compare more than two things, add "–est" to an adjective. Use an adjective to complete this sentence:

This is the _____ movie I've ever seen!

You can also add most or least before an adjective or adverb. Use an adverb to complete this sentence:

He walked the most _____ of anyone.

Switching Adjectives and Adverbs

What's wrong with the following sentences?

The sun shone bright.

The radio is loudly than the television.

What Makes a Sentence

A complete sentence always contains two parts:

- **Subject**
  The person or thing that the sentence is about.

- **Predicate**
  Tells what the subject does.

A group of words containing a subject and a predicate is called a clause.

What's the difference between this set of clauses…

> You should hurry.
> My shirt is blue.
> The cat is furious.

…and this set?

> unless you want to be late
> although my pants are not
> because he missed his nap

Putting Clauses Together

Here are some ways to join clauses to form sentences:

- Join a dependent clause and an independent clause, sometimes with a comma.

Try joining these clauses to make a sentence:

Dependent clause: because he missed the bus
Independent clause: he is late

- Join two independent clauses with a comma and a joining word.

Try joining these clauses to make a sentence:

Independent clause: my pen is out of ink
Independent clause: I need another one

- Join two independent clauses with a semicolon (;).

Try joining these clauses to make a sentence:

Independent clause: the phone is ringing
Independent clause: it won't stop

Practice Set 1

Solve the following questions based on what you've learned so far.

1. The natural habitat of the Komodo dragon is now <u>protected the animal</u> was formerly in danger of extinction.

(A) protected the animal
(B) protected, the animal
(C) protected; the animal
(D) protected which, the animal
(E) protected, thus functioning to make sure the animal

2. Ever since the discovery of <u>ancient ruins</u> in a local park,
                              A

our <u>extreme small town</u> has <u>become one</u> of the
        B   C

<u>most famous</u> locations in the area. <u>No error</u>
   D   E

3. Like most of the athletes in this race, <u>long-distance running is April's greatest strength</u>.

(A) long-distance running is April's greatest strength
(B) long-distance running being April's greatest strength
(C) April excels at long-distance running
(D) for whom long-distance running is a strength, like April
(E) being that long-distance running is the greatest strength of April

Punctuation

Comma Errors

The most common type of punctuation error you'll find on the SAT is the comma error. Here are the most common ones:

Missing Commas: Commas are needed to set off introductory phrases and extra (descriptive) information. They are also needed to separate items on lists, and they come before joining words (such as "and," "but," and "or").

Extra Commas: A comma should never fall in the middle of a phrase—for example, between a noun and its verb.

Comma Splices: A comma cannot separate two phrases that stand on their own as individual sentences. Only a semicolon can do that.

Can you spot the comma errors in the following sentences?

One of the country's leading experts on viruses the doctor lectured frequently.

The museum, scheduled several new exhibits for the spring.

There are many reasons to exercise regularly, improving your health is one of them.

Using Semicolons

Another type of punctuation question to look out for on the SAT is the semicolon question. What functions do the semicolons in the following two sentences serve?

There were several theories about why the project had failed; only one was correct.

In order to complete the project, they needed several buckets of paint; small, medium, and large brushes; and a tarp to cover the ground.

Note: Photocopying any part of this book is prohibited by law.

230

Passive Voice

What's the difference between these two sentences?

> The ball was thrown by the girl.
> The girl threw the ball.

On the SAT, correct sentences use the active voice. The passive voice is always incorrect.

Correct the following sentences.

> The man was bitten by a dog.

> The airplane was flown by the pilot.

> Many ideas were discussed by the students.

Noun Agreement

Sometimes related nouns need to match in number. Read carefully. If the first noun in a sentence is plural, think about whether the second one needs to be, as well.

Take a look at this sentence:

The people on my street take good care of their house.

What's wrong with it? Rewrite it correctly.

Practice Questions: Set 2

Use the concepts you've learned so far to solve these practice questions.

4. In the morning, <u>reports were given by four of the students</u> about the books they had read.

(A) reports were given by four of the students
(B) by four of the students reports were given
(C) reports by four of the students were given
(D) of the students, four giving reports
(E) four of the students gave reports

5. The <u>team, practiced every day</u> in the hopes of competing in the city-wide tournament.

(A) team, practiced every day
(B) team, practiced, every day
(C) team practiced, every day
(D) team practiced, every day,
(E) team practiced every day

6. The <u>students, preparing</u> for the school <u>play</u>, carefully <u>memorized</u> their <u>part</u>. <u>No error</u>
            A   B   C   D   E

Summary

In this unit, you leaned that:

- comparisons in sentences must compare like things.

- adjectives describe things; adverbs describe actions.

- complete sentences contain a subject and a predicate.

- there are numerous ways that commas may be misused in SAT Writing questions.

- on the SAT, active voice is correct and passive voice is incorrect.

- sometimes related nouns need to agree in number.

Answer Key

1. C
2. B
3. C
4. E
5. E
6. D

Session 8: Geometry Fundamentals II

In this unit, you will learn to:

- find the distance around a circle.

- find the area of a circle.

- find the surface area of solid figures.

- find the volume of solid figures.

Circles

Most of the circle questions will include figures. However, some won't, and you'll have to draw diagrams for yourself.

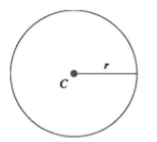

Extending from point C is a line that reaches to the edge of the circle. This line is called the radius of the circle.

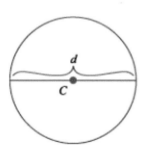

A diameter is basically a double radius that runs through the center of the circle and touches two points on the circle's edge.

A diameter is twice a radius.

In the same way, a radius is half a diameter.

Note: Photocopying any part of this book is prohibited by law.

236

Circles: Circumference

The formulas for the circumference and area of a circle involve the value pi, denoted by the following Greek letter: π.

The value of Pi, pronounced "pie," is approximately 3.14.

The circumference of a circle is the distance around its outer edge.

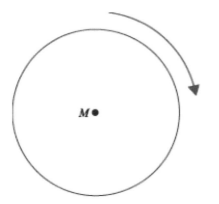

The formula for determining the circumference of a circle is: $C = 2\pi r$.

Since two radii make up one diameter, you may also see the formula for circumference expressed as: $C = \pi d$.

If the circumference of a circle is 14π, what does the radius of the circle measure? _____

Circles: Area

Look at circle Q. The shaded portion of circle Q is the area of the circle.

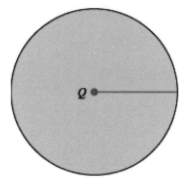

Here's the formula for the area of a circle:

$$A = \pi r^2$$

If the area of a circle is $100\,\pi$, what does the radius of the circle measure?

_____

Radius, Diameter, Circumference and Area

Fill in the missing values in the table below.

Radius	Diameter	Circumference	Area
3			
		12π	
			64π
	10		

Circles: Practice Questions

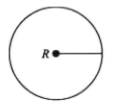

1. Circle R has a radius of 4. What is the circumference of circle R?

(A) 2π
(B) 4π
(C) 8π
(D) 16π
(E) 4

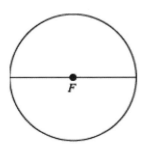

2. If circle F has an area of 36π, what is its diameter?

(A) 72
(B) 36
(C) 12
(D) 6
(E) 3

3. What is the circumference of a circle with area 25π?

(A) 2π
(B) 5π
(C) 10π
(D) 15π
(E) 25π

Solids

Solids are 3-D versions of regular shapes.

Cube

Cubes are the three-dimensional versions of squares. Each face of a cube is a square, so six identical squares make up a cube.

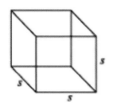

Rectangular Solid

Rectangular solids, which are shaped like boxes, are the 3-D versions of rectangles. Because each face is a rectangle, six rectangles make up a rectangular solid.

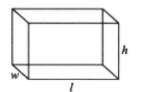

Cylinder

Cylinders are shaped like tin cans. The top and bottom faces are equal, parallel circles. A rectangle wraps around the circumference of these circles to form the tube that joins them.

Cylinders have two important dimensions: base and height. The base is the diameter of the circle, and the height is the distance the circles are apart.

Solids: Surface Area

The surface area of a solid figure is the sum of the areas of its faces.

Cubes

A cube is made up of 6 identical squares. Its surface area is the total area of these squares.

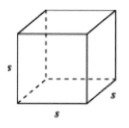

To find the area of a square, you multiply one side by another side: $s \times s$. So to find the surface area of a cube, you multiply the area of one square by six for the six faces. That gives you the formula:

$$6 \times s \times s.$$

If a side of a cube measures 5, what is its surface area? _____

Rectangular solids

Like a cube, a rectangular solid has six faces. Unlike a cube, however, a rectangular solid does not have six equal sides. But opposite sides are equal.

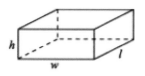

The area of two opposite rectangles is $l \times w$. The area of two other opposite rectangles is $l \times h$. The area of the final two opposite rectangles is $h \times w$.

So, the surface area of a rectangular solid is:

$$2(l \times w) + 2(l \times h) + 2(h \times w)$$

If a rectangular solid has a width of 4, a height of 5 and a length of 6, what is its surface area?

_____

Solids: Volume

Cubes

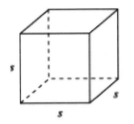

The formula for the volume of a cube is: $s \times s \times s$.

If a side of a cube measures 6, what is its volume? _____

Rectangular solids

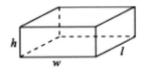

The volume of a rectangular solid is: $l \times w \times h$.

If a rectangular solid has a width of 3, a height of 4 and a length of 5, what is its volume? _____

Cylinders

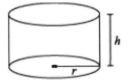

The volume of a cylinder is: $(\pi r^2) \times h$.

If a cylinder has a radius of 6 and a height of 8, what is its volume?

_____

Solids: Practice Questions

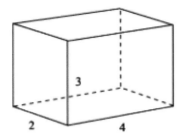

4. What is the surface area of the rectangular solid above?

(A) 12
(B) 24
(C) 48
(D) 52
(E) 64

5. The volume of a rectangular prism is 600 in^3. If its height measures 10 inches and its length measures 15 inches, what is the measure of its width, in inches?

(A) 90,000
(B) 90
(C) 40
(D) 5
(E) 4

6. Cube X has sides of length 3. Cube Y has sides that are twice as long as the sides of Cube X. What is the volume of Cube Y?

(A) 27
(B) 54
(C) 81
(D) 162
(E) 216

Summary

In this unit, you learned that:

- a diameter of a circle is twice its radius.

- the formula for the circumference of a circle is $C = 2\pi r$ or πd.

- the formula for the area of a circle is $A = \pi r^2$.

- there are three important solid figures to know: cubes, rectangular solids, and cylinders.

- the surface area of a solid figure equals the sum of the areas of its faces.

- the volume of a solid figure equals the area of its base times its height.

Answer Key

1. C
2. C
3. C
4. D
5. E
6. E

Session 8: Geometry Strategy

In this unit, you will learn:

- to look for the "Usual Suspects" triangles that come up again and again on the SAT.

- how to use diagrams.

- how to approach problems with multiple geometric shapes.

The Usual Suspects

The triangles below appear frequently on the SAT, and often in disguise. Sometimes they appear in questions with multiple geometric figures, and sometimes they appear in questions where the figure is not drawn to scale.

The first pair of triangles is characterized by equal angles and equal sides.

Suspect 1: The Isosceles Triangle

Two sides are equal. The angles opposite the equal sides are always equal.

If the two equal angles of an isosceles triangle each measure 70 degrees, what does the remaining angle measure?

_____

Suspect 2: The Equilateral Triangle

All three sides are equal. All three angles are also equal; they each measure 60 degrees.

If the perimeter of an isosceles triangle is 27, what does each of the sides measure?

_____

Suspect 3: The Isosceles Right Triangle

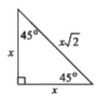

Also known as a 45-45-90 triangle since its angle measures are 45°, 45°, and 90°.

The two shorter sides (legs) are equal, and the longer side (hypotenuse) is equal to the length of a leg times $\sqrt{2}$ (according to the Pythagorean Theorem). Its side lengths, therefore, have a ratio of $x : x : x\sqrt{2}$.

What is the area of a 45-45-90 right triangle whose hypotenuse measures $8\sqrt{2}$?

_____

Suspect 4: The 30-60-90 Right Triangle

Its angle measures are 30°, 60°, and 90°. It pays to memorize the relationship between the shorter leg, the longer leg, and the hypotenuse: $x : x\sqrt{3} : 2x$.

If two sides of a 30-60-90 right triangle measure 3 and 6, what does the remaining side measure?

_____

Suspect 5: The 3-4-5 Right Triangle

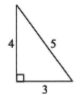

Can you name some other triangles whose sides have a 3:4:5 ratio?

_____
_____
_____

Suspect 6: The 5-12-13 Right Triangle

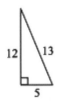

Like the 3-4-5 triangle, the 5-12-13 triangle may appear in disguise. Name some other triangles whose sides have a 5:12:13 ratio.

_____
_____
_____

Looking for the Usual Suspects

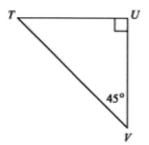

1. What is the area of triangle *TUV* above if *TU* = 6?

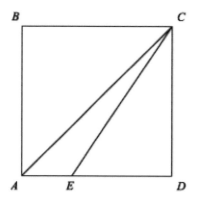

2. In the figure above, triangle *ACE* is inscribed in square *ABCD*. If the area of the square is 144, and $AE = \frac{1}{3}ED$, what is the length of *EC*?

(A) 12
(B) $8\sqrt{2}$
(C) $8\sqrt{3}$
(D) 15
(E) $12\sqrt{2}$

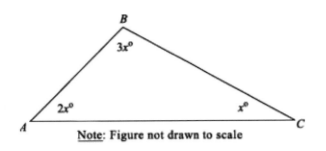

Note: Figure not drawn to scale

3. What is the perimeter of triangle *ABC* above if *AC* = 20?

(A) $30 + 10\sqrt{2}$
(B) $30 + 10\sqrt{3}$
(C) $40 + 10\sqrt{3}$
(D) $40\sqrt{2}$
(E) $50\sqrt{2}$

Note: Photocopying any part of this book is prohibited by law.

250

Using Diagrams

Knowing how to use a diagram can help you with geometry questions on the SAT.

Drawn to Scale

Unless otherwise stated, all geometry diagrams are drawn to scale. When the figure is drawn to scale, you can:

- use it to "eyeball" the value you are looking for and eliminate unlikely answer choices.

- write information provided in the question directly on the figure to help you to answer the question.

Look at the following figure and the accompanying "nonsense question." Which choices can you eliminate just from eyeballing this figure which is drawn to scale?

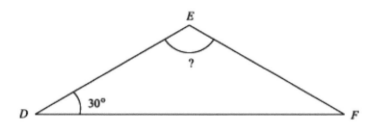

4. What is the measure of angle E?

(A) 40
(B) 60
(C) 90
(D) 110
(E) 120

Using Diagrams (continued)

For this advanced question, just list two choices that you can eliminate by eyeballing the figure:

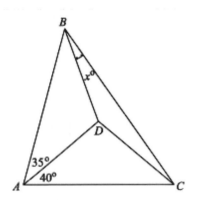

5. In the figure above $AD = BD = DC$. What is the value of x?

(A) 12.5
(B) 15
(C) 20
(D) 30
(E) 40

_____ and _____ MUST be wrong.

Not Drawn to Scale

When the figure is not drawn to scale:

- you cannot use it to "eyeball" the value you are looking for and eliminate unlikely answer choices.

- redraw the figure to reflect the information in the question.

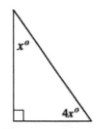

Note: Figure not drawn to scale

6. In the right triangle above, what is the value of x?

(A) 15
(B) 18
(C) 22.5
(D) 30
(E) 36

No Figure at All

When no figure is provided, draw your own figure!

7. A rectangle has a perimeter of 28. If one of its sides is equal to 8, what is the length of its diagonal?

Shared Lines and Angles

Many hard geometry questions involve multiple geometric shapes that overlap or are inscribed in one another. The key to solving these problems is finding the line or angle that is shared by both figures.

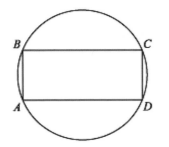

8. In the figure above, rectangle *ABCD* is inscribed in a circle. If *AB* = 10 and the area of rectangle *ABCD* is 240, what is the area of the circle?

(A) 144π
(B) 169π
(C) 196π
(D) 225π
(E) 256π

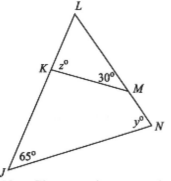

Note: Figure not drawn to scale

9. In the figure above, what is the value of *z* in terms of *y*?

(A) $180 - y$
(B) $145 - y$
(C) $y + 15$
(D) $y + 35$
(E) $y + 50$

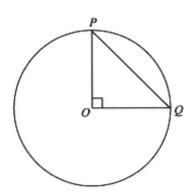

10. If the area of circle O above is 9π, what is the length of PQ?

(A) 3
(B) $2\sqrt{3}$
(C) $3\sqrt{2}$
(D) $3\sqrt{3}$
(E) 6

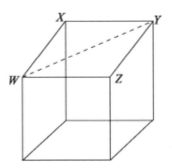

11. In the cube above, the measure of WY is $3\sqrt{2}$. What is the volume of the cube?

(A) 3
(B) $3\sqrt{2}$
(C) 9
(D) 27
(E) $27\sqrt{2}$

Summary

In this unit, you learned that:

- "Usual Suspects" triangles commonly appear on the SAT, sometimes in disguise.

- sometimes you should use the provided diagram, and sometimes you should make your own.

- on problems that involve overlapping figures, you should look for shared lines or angles.

Answer Key

1. 18
2. D
3. B
5. B
6. A
7. 10
8. B
9. D
10. C
11. D

Session 8: Sentence Improvement Strategy

In this unit, you will learn to:

- use strategies to solve Sentence Improvement questions.

- recognize common Sentence Improvement mistakes.

Sentence Improvement Overview

In the Sentence Improvement section of the test, you'll see questions that look something like this:

1. Despite the equipment malfunctions that the team encountered at the beginning of the project, <u>the work taking less time</u> than everyone had expected.

(A) the work taking less time
(B) the work took less time
(C) and the work taking less time
(D) the time of the work is less
(E) the work was timed less

The underlined part may contain a mistake, but it doesn't always. The answer choices are all different versions of the underlined part. Your job is to determine whether one of the answer choices is better than the original underlined portion. If the original is best, you'll select choice (A), which is the same version that appears in the question.

Solving Sentence Improvement Questions

Follow this method to solve Sentence Improvement questions:

1) **Read the entire sentence.** As you do, try to determine the construction employed in the underlined portion. For example, does it contain a verb phrase? A description?

2) **Determine whether the underlined portion contains a mistake.** Even if you're pretty sure the original version is correct, it's a good idea to skim the choices to make sure.

3) **Evaluate the choices.** Don't waste time reading choice (A)—it's always the same as the underlined portion. You don't always need to read each choice in its entirety. Instead, look for the differences among the choices. That'll point you to where the mistake is.

Now try to solve this Sentence Improvement question.

1. Despite the equipment malfunctions that the team encountered at the beginning of the project, <u>the work taking less time</u> than everyone had expected.

(A) the work taking less time
(B) the work took less time
(C) and the work taking less time
(D) the time of the work is less
(E) the work was timed less

Look for the split. Sometimes the answer choices are split in style. In other words, two of the choices change one aspect of the sentence, while two change another. If you know what's wrong with the sentence, you can eliminate two choices at once.

Common Sentence Improvement Errors

While Sentence Improvement questions cover a wide range of material, there are some mistakes that show up often:

Clause Structure

What's the problem with this sentence?

> The crowd was overwhelmingly enthusiastic, the singer performed an encore.

Connecting Words

Can you figure out what's wrong with this sentence and rewrite it correctly?

> The teacher often had the students correct each other's essays, and it was an exercise in grammar.

Modifiers

Underline the modifier in this sentence. Can you rewrite the sentence to make it clearer?

> The grapes grew in a few regions, which were purple.

Wordiness

Cross out the extra words in the following sentence.

> The girls enjoyed playing sports; of which their favorite was soccer.

Choice (A)

The original sentence won't always have an error—sometimes choice (A) is correct. Expect that choice (A) will be the correct answer to at least one Sentence Improvement question. However, don't get lazy and blindly select choice (A); for the majority of questions, it won't be the correct answer. Before you select choice (A):

1. Read the original sentence carefully and think about common mistakes.

2. Ask yourself if the sentence is written as clearly and simply as possible.

3. Read each answer choice carefully. If you're focus on just one word, you might not notice another change the choice introduces.

Practice Questions

Use the concepts you've learned so far to solve these practice questions.

2. Not only will the musicians perform several period pieces, <u>and they will also explain the history of the music</u>.

(A) and they will also explain the history of the music
(B) and, too, they will be explaining the history of the music
(C) also will be explaining the history of the music
(D) they will also explain the history of the music
(E) explaining also the history of the music

3. <u>The book club read one book each month that the group leader chose, and</u> then met to discuss it.

(A) The book club read one book each month that the group leader chose, and
(B) The book club read one book each month, choosing the group leader, and
(C) The book club read one book for each month that was chosen by the group leader,
(D) Each month, the book club read one book that the group leader chose, and
(E) Each month, chosen by the group leader, the book club read one book,

4. <u>A classical cellist, Yo-Yo Ma has also experimented</u> with other types of music, including Brazilian and American bluegrass.

(A) A classical cellist, Yo-Yo Ma has also experimented
(B) A classical cellist, experiments by Yo-Yo Ma include working
(C) Yo-Yo Ma, being a classical cellist, experimenting
(D) The experimentation of a classical cellist, Yo-Yo Ma did
(E) A classical cellist, the music of Yo-Yo Ma has experimented

5. The natural habitat of the chimpanzee has largely been <u>destroyed that puts</u> the animals in great danger.

(A) destroyed that puts
(B) destroyed, that puts
(C) destroyed; that puts
(D) destroyed which, is putting
(E) destroyed, thus functioning to put

6. Although the artists had very different ideas of how the mural should look, <u>they worked together which was to create</u> a single painting that united their visions.

(A) they worked together which was to create
(B) and yet they worked together which was to create
(C) and they worked together which was to create
(D) they worked together they created
(E) they worked together to create

Summary

In this unit, you learned that:

- Sentence Improvement questions contain an underlined piece that may or may not contain a mistake.

- choice (A) is always the same as the underlined part of the sentence.

- common errors to look for include misplaced modifiers, incorrect clause structure, wordiness, and misused connecting words.

- in evaluating answer choices, you should look for a split and eliminate like choices that you know do not correct the mistake.

Answer Key

1. B
2. D
3. D
4. A
5. C
6. E

Session 8: Paired Passages

In this unit, you will learn to:

- identify Paired Passages.

- recognize what Paired Passages test.

- use Peterson's technique for Paired Passages.

Paired Passages: The Basics

Paired Passages are two passages written by different authors on a related subject or theme. The ideas in one passage will agree or disagree with the other.

Long Paired Passages

Long Paired Passages usually follow this structure:

The two passages are presented first.
The first questions in the set ask about Passage 1.
The next block of questions asks about Passage 2.
The last few questions ask you to compare and contrast the passages.

Short Paired Passages

How do Short Paired Passages differ from Long Paired Passages?

The Peterson's Technique for Long Paired Passages

Here's how to approach Long Paired Passages:

- Build on what you know.
- Choose Passage 1 or 2.
- Use Peterson's technique for Critical Reading.
- Repeat for the other passage.
- Answer the Comparison questions last.

How should you approach Short Paired Passages?

Note: Photocopying any part of this book is prohibited by law.

266

About Comparison Questions

The group of Comparison questions that usually appears at the end of the question set is what sets Paired Passages apart from other reading passages. These questions fall into a few predictable categories:

General Comparison

Some Comparison questions are based on a general understanding of what each passage says. They ask about things such as:

How are the two viewpoints similar?
How are they different?
What do both authors assume?
What is the main point of the two passages?
What in the passages is contradictory?

Detail Relationship

Other Comparison questions ask you how a detail in one passage relates to some element of the other passage. For example, suppose Passage 1 is a scientific discussion about chimp language skills and Passage 2 is a narrative from an anthropologist teaching a chimp to talk.

What might a Detail Relationship Comparison question ask you in regard to these two passages?

_____

_____

Passage Approach

A third type of Comparison question asks you to compare the approaches taken by the authors. For example:

What similarities are there in the approaches employed by the two authors?
What differences are there in the two approaches?
How does the general tone of one passage compare with that of the other?

Note: Photocopying any part of this book is prohibited by law.

267

Choosing a Passage

Read the passages below. Which one would you choose to handle first? Why?

Passage 1 is an excerpt from an early twentieth-century account of the life and philosophy of Henry David Thoreau. Passage 2 discusses a late twentieth-century movement called Voluntary Simplicity.

Passage 1

Early nineteenth-century New England straddled a fence between the decaying medieval civilization of its inheritance and the bustling industrial juggernaut coming into being. Henry David Thoreau was perhaps the only man who paused to give a report of the full experience. In a period when men were on the move, he remained still; when men
5 were on the make, he remained poor. Thoreau, in his life and letters, shows what the pioneer movement might have come to if this great migration had sought culture rather than material conquest, and an intensity of life, rather than mere extension over the continent.
Whereas his fellow townsman Emerson cleared out of his mind every idea that made no
10 direct connections with his personal experience, Thoreau cleared out of his life itself every custom or physical apparatus, to boot, which could not stand up and justify its existence…

Passage 2

Phone ringing off the hook, TV blaring non-stop, products scattered everywhere, overdue credit card bills, mounting stress, two jobs to keep it all afloat... It is no
40 coincidence that the increasing pressure on Americans to keep up with the incessant, ever-accelerating drumbeat of modern life has been accompanied by a resurgence in the "voluntary simplicity" movement. Begun as an off-shoot of the environmental movement of the 1970s, voluntary simplicity stresses a return to simple, genuine living, unencumbered as best as possible by the myriad material contrivances that impinge upon
45 our lives. It involves a conscious decision to reduce clutter, both physical and mental. Voluntary simplicity is not about denying oneself the pleasures of life, but rather replacing mediocre pleasures with better ones. It is about trying to live more deliberately…

Note: Photocopying any part of this book is prohibited by law.

268

Tackling Passage 2

Read the first half of Passage 2 and answer Questions 6 and 7 (the first two questions about it in the set).

Passage 1 is an excerpt from an early twentieth-century account of the life and philosophy of Henry David Thoreau. Passage 2 discusses a late twentieth-century movement called Voluntary Simplicity.

Passage 2

    Phone ringing off the hook, TV blaring non-stop, products scattered everywhere, overdue credit card bills, mounting stress, two jobs to keep it all afloat... It is no
40 coincidence that the increasing pressure on Americans to keep up with the incessant, ever-accelerating drumbeat of modern life has been accompanied by a resurgence in the "voluntary simplicity" movement. Begun as an off-shoot of the environmental movement of the 1970s, voluntary simplicity stresses a return to simple, genuine living, unencumbered as best as possible by the myriad material contrivances that impinge upon
45 our lives. It involves a conscious decision to reduce clutter, both physical and mental. Voluntary simplicity is not about denying oneself the pleasures of life, but rather replacing mediocre pleasures with better ones. It is about trying to live more deliberately…

6. In Passage 2, "the incessant, ever-accelerating drumbeat of modern life" (lines 40-41) refers to the

(A) excitement of living in the modern world
(B) increasingly complicated lives people lead
(C) regular rhythm of current events
(D) traditions of a bygone era
(E) expectation of others leading technological lives

7. The author of Passage 2 implies which of the following about the environmental movement of the 1970s (lines 42-45)?

(A) Without it few people would have considered the idea of simple living.
(B) It has continued to grow until the present day.
(C) It drew energy from the voluntary simplicity movement.
(D) Its goal was consistent with the premises of voluntary simplicity.
(E) Its success depended on people denying themselves the basic amenities of modern life.

Continuing with Passage 2

Next you would tackle Questions 8 and 9, using the questions to guide you to the relevant parts of the passage.

Passage 1 is an excerpt from an early twentieth-century account of the life and philosophy of Henry David Thoreau. Passage 2 discusses a late twentieth-century movement called Voluntary Simplicity.

Passage 2

Phone ringing off the hook, TV blaring non-stop, products scattered everywhere, overdue credit card bills, mounting stress, two jobs to keep it all afloat... It is no
40 coincidence that the increasing pressure on Americans to keep up with the incessant, ever-accelerating drumbeat of modern life has been accompanied by a resurgence in the "voluntary simplicity" movement. Begun as an off-shoot of the environmental movement of the 1970s, voluntary simplicity stresses a return to simple, genuine living, unencumbered as best as possible by the myriad material contrivances that impinge upon
45 our lives. It involves a conscious decision to reduce clutter, both physical and mental. Voluntary simplicity is not about denying oneself the pleasures of life, but rather replacing mediocre pleasures with better ones. It is about trying to live more deliberately.
For some, the move towards simplicity is financially motivated; for others, it is born
50 out of the desire to flee the corporate "rat race." People who are not obsessed with trying to "get ahead" gain a tremendous amount of freedom to speak their mind with impunity. They minimize their financial needs in order to spend as much time and energy as possible in more meaningful activities such as connecting with other humans, pursuing intellectual growth, and giving service to causes for which they have a passion. Less time
55 spent keeping track of, organizing, insuring, protecting, showing off, and maintaining things, leaves more time to spend with family, friends, and children. A common refrain throughout the movement is the desire to spend time living instead of making a living. To its adherents, voluntary simplicity is about freedom—about taking ownership of one's own life.
60 Many who practice voluntary simplicity today were one-time diehard consumerists who, for one reason or another, turned their back on their former lifestyles. Ideologically, the two groups stand in direct opposition. Consumerists scoff at the naiveté of "voluntary simpletons" haughtily attempting to live without the normal amenities of modern life. Most practitioners of voluntary simplicity view consumerists as unenlightened trend—
65 followers lured by false promises of material pleasures. The more militant see consumerists as outright threats to a sustainable economy.

8. In line 56, "refrain" most nearly means

(A) song
(B) withholding
(C) theme
(D) joke
(E) challenge

9. In Passage 2, the phrase "voluntary simpletons" (lines 62-63) is used to convey what attitude on the part of consumerists?

(A) respect for the practitioners of voluntary simplicity
(B) puzzlement over the goals and methods of voluntary simplicity
(C) scorn for the notion of voluntary simplicity
(D) anger at the effect the voluntary simplicity movement is having on the economy
(E) admiration for the high level of commitment necessary to maintain a life of voluntary simplicity

Note: Photocopying any part of this book is prohibited by law.

271

Deciding How to Proceed

Suppose after Question 9, you see the following for Question 10:

> 10. Thoreau and the modern adherents of voluntary simplicity share

What do you notice about this question?

Now suppose you see this for Question 1:

> 1. Both passages are primarily concerned with

How do you handle this?

Moving on, say that you see the following for Question 2:

> 2. In context, the phrase "straddled a fence" (line 2) signifies that early nineteenth-century New England

Should you try this one?

Note: Photocopying any part of this book is prohibited by law.

273

Tackling Passage 1

You would next read the first half of Passage 1 and answer the questions that pertain to it.

Passage 1 is an excerpt from an early twentieth-century account of the life and philosophy of Henry David Thoreau. Passage 2 discusses a late twentieth-century movement called Voluntary Simplicity.

Passage 1

Early nineteenth-century New England straddled a fence between the decaying medieval civilization of its inheritance and the bustling industrial juggernaut coming into being. Henry David Thoreau was perhaps the only man who paused to give a report of the full experience. In a period when men were on the move, he remained still; when men
5 were on the make, he remained poor. Thoreau, in his life and letters, shows what the pioneer movement might have come to if this great migration had sought culture rather than material conquest, and an intensity of life, rather than mere extension over the continent.

Whereas his fellow townsman Emerson cleared out of his mind every idea that made no
10 direct connections with his personal experience, Thoreau cleared out of his life itself every custom or physical apparatus, to boot, which could not stand up and justify its existence. "A native of the United States," de Tocqueville had observed, "clings to the world's goods as if he were certain never to die; and he is so hasty at grasping at all within his reach that one would suppose he was constantly afraid of not living long
15 enough to enjoy them. He clutches everything, he holds nothing fast, but soon loosens his grasp to pursue fresh gratifications." Thoreau completely reversed this process: it was because he wanted to live fully that he turned away from everything that did not serve toward this end. He prized the minutes for what they brought, and would not fill his hours with gainful practices beyond what was needed for the bare business of keeping his
20 bodily self warm and active...

2. In context, the phrase "straddled a fence" (line 1) signifies that early nineteenth-century New England

(A) was stagnating economically
(B) was paralyzed by indecision
(C) was experiencing a transition
(D) was populated by people wary of the emerging industrial society
(E) was the first region in the United States to break with its medieval past

3. The author cites the quote by de Tocqueville in lines 12-16 ("A native of...fresh gratifications") primarily in order to

(A) illuminate an attitude that will serve as a contrast
(B) introduce de Tocqueville's ideas on political philosophy
(C) refute an earlier assertion
(D) evaluate the mentality that dominated American life in the nineteenth century
(E) emphasize the impracticality of Emerson's position

4. In line 15, "fast" most nearly means

(A) obediently
(B) quick
(C) purposely
(D) firm
(E) sacred

Moving through Passage 1

The whole passage is now included for you. Proceed with Question 5.

Passage 1

Early nineteenth-century New England straddled a fence between the decaying medieval civilization of its inheritance and the bustling industrial juggernaut coming into being. Henry David Thoreau was perhaps the only man who paused to give a report of the full experience. In a period when men were on the move, he remained still; when men
5   were on the make, he remained poor. Thoreau, in his life and letters, shows what the pioneer movement might have come to if this great migration had sought culture rather than material conquest, and an intensity of life, rather than mere extension over the continent.

    Whereas his fellow townsman Emerson cleared out of his mind every idea that made no
10   direct connections with his personal experience, Thoreau cleared out of his life itself every custom or physical apparatus, to boot, which could not stand up and justify its existence. "A native of the United States," de Tocqueville had observed, "clings to the world's goods as if he were certain never to die; and he is so hasty at grasping at all within his reach that one would suppose he was constantly afraid of not living long
15   enough to enjoy them. He clutches everything, he holds nothing fast, but soon loosens his grasp to pursue fresh gratifications." Thoreau completely reversed this process: it was because he wanted to live fully that he turned away from everything that did not serve toward this end. He prized the minutes for what they brought, and would not fill his hours with gainful practices beyond what was needed for the bare business of keeping his
20   bodily self warm and active. Speaking of the business culture that had by the 1850s begun to dominate all aspects of American life, Thoreau wrote: "I think that there is nothing, not even crime, more opposed to poetry, to philosophy, ay, to life itself, than this incessant business... The ways by which you may get money almost without exception lead downward. To have done anything by which you have earned money
25   merely is to have been truly idle or worse."

    Thoreau seized the opportunity to consider what in its essentials a truly human life was; he sought to find out what degree of food, clothing, shelter, and labor was necessary to sustain it. He discovered that people are so eager to get the ostentatious "necessaries" of a civil life that they lose the opportunity to profit by civilization itself: while their physical
30   wants are complicated, their lives, culturally, are not enriched in proportion, but are rather pauperized and bleached. Thoreau lived in his desires. The pioneer, by contrast, lived only in extraneous necessities. Filling his world with objects of conquest—land, goods, and countless diversions—he never fulfilled himself. Beginning with the same initial feeling toward Nature, Thoreau and the pioneer stood at opposite corners of the
35   field. What Thoreau left behind is still precious; men may still go out and make over America in the image of Thoreau. What the pioneer left behind, alas! was only the burden of a vacant life.

5. The author of Passage 1 believes that "a vacant life" (line 37) results from

(A) calculating how much food, clothing, shelter and labor is necessary for a truly human life
(B) cultivating the spiritual side of one's personality
(C) desiring to explore new lands
(D) admitting the necessity of satisfying physical wants
(E) sacrificing culture in favor of material satisfactions

Note: Photocopying any part of this book is prohibited by law.

277

Tackling the Comparison Questions

Now it's time to tackle the Comparison questions. Start with Question 1, and then move on to 10-12. As you work on each question, think about whether it is a General Comparison, Detail Relationship, or Passage Approach question.

Passage 1

Early nineteenth-century New England straddled a fence between the decaying medieval civilization of its inheritance and the bustling industrial juggernaut coming into being. Henry David Thoreau was perhaps the only man who paused to give a report of the full experience. In a period when men were on the move, he remained still; when men
5 were on the make, he remained poor. Thoreau, in his life and letters, shows what the pioneer movement might have come to if this great migration had sought culture rather than material conquest, and an intensity of life, rather than mere extension over the continent.

Whereas his fellow townsman Emerson cleared out of his mind every idea that made no
10 direct connections with his personal experience, Thoreau cleared out of his life itself every custom or physical apparatus, to boot, which could not stand up and justify its existence. "A native of the United States," de Tocqueville had observed, "clings to the world's goods as if he were certain never to die; and he is so hasty at grasping at all within his reach that one would suppose he was constantly afraid of not living long
15 enough to enjoy them. He clutches everything, he holds nothing fast, but soon loosens his grasp to pursue fresh gratifications." Thoreau completely reversed this process: it was because he wanted to live fully that he turned away from everything that did not serve toward this end. He prized the minutes for what they brought, and would not fill his hours with gainful practices beyond what was needed for the bare business of keeping his
20 bodily self warm and active. Speaking of the business culture that had by the 1850s begun to dominate all aspects of American life, Thoreau wrote: "I think that there is nothing, not even crime, more opposed to poetry, to philosophy, ay, to life itself, than this incessant business... The ways by which you may get money almost without exception lead downward. To have done anything by which you have earned money
25 merely is to have been truly idle or worse."

Thoreau seized the opportunity to consider what in its essentials a truly human life was; he sought to find out what degree of food, clothing, shelter, and labor was necessary to sustain it. He discovered that people are so eager to get the ostentatious "necessaries" of a civil life that they lose the opportunity to profit by civilization itself: while their physical
30 wants are complicated, their lives, culturally, are not enriched in proportion, but are rather pauperized and bleached. Thoreau lived in his desires. The pioneer, by contrast, lived only in extraneous necessities. Filling his world with objects of conquest—land, goods, and countless diversions—he never fulfilled himself. Beginning with the same initial feeling toward Nature, Thoreau and the pioneer stood at opposite corners of the
35 field. What Thoreau left behind is still precious; men may still go out and make over America in the image of Thoreau. What the pioneer left behind, alas! was only the burden of a vacant life.

Passage 2

    Phone ringing off the hook, TV blaring non-stop, products scattered everywhere, overdue credit card bills, mounting stress, two jobs to keep it all afloat... It is no
40 coincidence that the increasing pressure on Americans to keep up with the incessant, ever-accelerating drumbeat of modern life has been accompanied by a resurgence in the "voluntary simplicity" movement. Begun as an off-shoot of the environmental movement of the 1970s, voluntary simplicity stresses a return to simple, genuine living, unencumbered as best as possible by the myriad material contrivances that impinge upon
45 our lives. It involves a conscious decision to reduce clutter, both physical and mental. Voluntary simplicity is not about denying oneself the pleasures of life, but rather replacing mediocre pleasures with better ones. It is about trying to live more deliberately.
    For some, the move towards simplicity is financially motivated; for others, it is born
50 out of the desire to flee the corporate "rat race." People who are not obsessed with trying to "get ahead" gain a tremendous amount of freedom to speak their mind with impunity. They minimize their financial needs in order to spend as much time and energy as possible in more meaningful activities such as connecting with other humans, pursuing intellectual growth, and giving service to causes for which they have a passion. Less time
55 spent keeping track of, organizing, insuring, protecting, showing off, and maintaining things, leaves more time to spend with family, friends, and children. A common refrain throughout the movement is the desire to spend time living instead of making a living. To its adherents, voluntary simplicity is about freedom—about taking ownership of one's own life.
60 Many who practice voluntary simplicity today were one-time diehard consumerists who, for one reason or another, turned their back on their former lifestyles. Ideologically, the two groups stand in direct opposition. Consumerists scoff at the naiveté of "voluntary simpletons" haughtily attempting to live without the normal amenities of modern life. Most practitioners of voluntary simplicity view consumerists as unenlightened trend—
65 followers lured by false promises of material pleasures. The more militant see consumerists as outright threats to a sustainable economy.

1. Both passages are primarily concerned with

(A) the struggle of individuals against the demands of business culture
(B) the methods by which one achieves financial independence
(C) the opposition between a simple life and one dominated by material concerns
(D) the philosophy of a particular historical figure
(E) the attitude necessary to bring about a sustainable economy

10. Thoreau and the modern adherents of voluntary simplicity share

(A) a desire to willfully organize their time and circumstances
(B) a willingness to enter the business culture if they can do so on their own terms
(C) a fear of material objects
(D) a deep disdain for most of their respective contemporaries
(E) a strong need to be alone

11. The consumerist of Passage 2 is most similar to which of the following from Passage 1?

(A) Thoreau
(B) Emerson
(C) the business culture
(D) the pioneer
(E) de Tocqueville

12. The approaches of the two passages differ in which of the following ways?

(A) Passage 1 suggests a negative effect of business culture.
(B) Passage 2 includes a description of contrasting viewpoints.
(C) Passage 2 provides a detailed historical account.
(D) Passage 2 offers an opinion of the author regarding a conflict described.
(E) Passage 1 contains a biographical sketch of an individual.

Summary

In this unit, you learned that:

- Paired Passages are two passages written by different authors on a related subject or theme.

- Paired Passages contain the same question types as other passages, with the addition of Comparison questions.

- to succeed on Long Paired Passages, you should use a slightly modified version of Peterson's Technique for Critical Reading.

- for Short Paired Passages, you should read both passages fully before proceeding to the questions.

- for Long Paired Passages, you should first work on the passage that seems easier for you, and save all of the Comparison questions for last.

- common Comparison question types are General Comparison, Detail Relationship, and Passage Approach.

Answer Key

6. B
7. D
8. C
9. C
2. C
3. A
4. D
5. E
1. C
10. A
11. D
12. E

Session 9: Arithmetic Strategy

In this unit, you will learn to:

- handle missing digits problems.

- correctly figure out the number of items in a counting question.

- deal with absolute value signs.

- avoid the wrong answers on least/greatest possible number questions.

- figure out the new average when you add or subtract values from a set.

- tackle tricky percent word problems.

- answer consecutive integers problems when you can't work backwards.

Missing Digits Problems

In these problems, a variable stands for one or more of the digits in an arithmetic problem. Think about what number must be added to the number shown in the column to result in the number in that column of the solution.

The key to these problems is remembering that sometimes you carry when you do addition.

$$
\begin{array}{r}
1\,x\,6 \\
+\quad x\,y \\
\hline
2\,3\,4
\end{array}
$$

1. In the above correctly worked addition problem, some digits have been replaced by the symbols x and y. What is the value of x?

(A) 1
(B) 2
(C) 4
(D) 5
(E) 6

Counting Questions

Counting questions ask you to count the numbers in a set, usually the set of numbers between two points. The key to these questions is subtracting the smaller number from the bigger and then adding 1.

Think about it. If you buy raffle tickets consecutively numbered from 1 to 5, you clearly have 5 tickets. If you simply subtract 1 from 5, you come up with 4 tickets. Therefore, you must add 1.

2. In a certain biology class, the lowest possible grade on the final exam was 55, and the highest possible grade, including extra credit, was 105. How many possible grades were there?

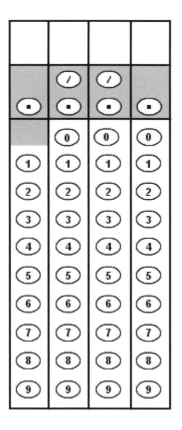

Absolute Value Questions

Absolute value is expressed by putting a number inside two vertical lines. The absolute value of x is written $|x|$.

- The absolute value of a number is its distance from zero.
- Absolute values are always positive.

$$|5| = |-5| = 5$$

3. $|-15| - |15| - |-15| =$

(A) -45
(B) -15
(C) 15
(D) 30
(E) 45

Be careful: While the absolute value of a number is always positive, the answer to an absolute value question doesn't have to be.

Least/Greatest Number Questions

Some questions ask you to find the least possible integer or greatest possible integer that fits a given description.

The key to these questions is knowing that the correct answer is rarely the biggest or smallest answer choice.

4. Set X contains all even integers between -5 and 20, inclusive. If S and T are distinct members of Set X, which of the following is the largest possible value of $T - S$?

(A) 13
(B) 15
(C) 20
(D) 24
(E) 25

Avoid the smallest answer choice in Least questions and the biggest answer choice in Greatest questions.

Note: Photocopying any part of this book is prohibited by law.

287

Adding to the Average Questions

Some average questions ask what happens to the average when a new term is added to or subtracted from the group.

The key to these questions is working with the sum of the original group of terms.

5. The average (arithmetic mean) weight of 8 melons in a display was 8.5 pounds. If a melon that weighed exactly 7.6 pounds were added to the display, what would be the new average (arithmetic mean) weight of the melons?

(A) 8.25
(B) 8.35
(C) 8.40
(D) 9.45
(E) 16.1

The following facts can help you eliminate choices:

- If the term added is smaller than the original average, the new average will be smaller; if it is bigger, then the new average will be bigger.

- If the term subtracted is smaller than the original average, the new average will be bigger; if it is bigger, then the new average will be smaller.

What choices can you eliminate from this question?

Note: Photocopying any part of this book is prohibited by law.

288

Tricky Percent Word Problems

Some percent word problems can trip you up because of the way they're worded. Watch the language. If you misidentify the part, whole, or percent, you'll come up with the wrong answer.

The key is remembering that the part is associated with the word "is," the whole is associated with the word "of," and the percent is associated with the percent sign, %.

6. 40 is 80% of what number?

(A) 32
(B) 40
(C) 48
(D) 50
(E) 120

Some questions seem hard because they include percents less than 1 or greater than 100. Follow the rules and you'll be fine.

7. What is 160% of 40?

(A) 0.25
(B) 4
(C) 25
(D) 64
(E) 400

Remember that 100% of a number is the number itself.

Note: Photocopying any part of this book is prohibited by law.

289

Sequence Questions

Sequence questions give you a sequence and then ask you to find the value of one or more terms in the sequence.

The key is identifying the pattern.

$$-1, 1, -1, -1, \ldots$$

8. The first two terms in the sequence of numbers shown above are -1 and 1. Each term in the sequence after the second is the result of dividing the term two terms before it by the term immediately before it. For example, the third term is $\dfrac{-1}{1}$ and the fourth term is $\dfrac{-1}{1}$. What is the sum of the 24th and 25th terms in this sequence?

(A) -2
(B) -1
(C) 0
(D) 1
(E) 2

Sometimes you aren't told that there's a pattern. Remember, the SAT isn't testing your ability to do tedious calculations. If it seems like that's what you need to do to solve, there must be a better way.

9. What is the units' digit of 3^{999}?

(A) 1
(B) 3
(C) 5
(D) 7
(E) 9

Hint: Try jotting down the first few powers of 3. How can this pattern help you solve the problem?

Consecutive Integers Problems: What If You Can't Work Backwards?

If a consecutive integers problem is a Grid-In, you can't work backwards from the answer choices. While you could use algebra to solve, there's often an easier way. See if you can use the following facts about the averages of consecutive integers to solve.

- The average of a group of consecutive integers is equal to its middle term.

- The average of a group of consecutive integers is equal to the average of its first and last terms.

10. A woman in the checkout line of a grocery store is holding a number of apples, and there are six women behind her, each with one more apple than the woman in front of her. If the seven women have a total of 84 apples, how many apples is the fourth woman holding?

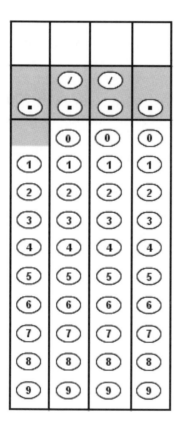

Note: Photocopying any part of this book is prohibited by law.

291

Summary

In this unit, you learned that:

- the key to missing digits questions is remembering that there may be carrying in addition.

- the key to counting questions is remembering to add 1 after subtracting the smaller number from the larger.

- absolute value is the distance a number is from zero and is therefore always positive. However, the answer to an absolute value question doesn't have to be positive.

- you should avoid the smallest answer choice in Least Possible Number questions and the largest answer choice in Greatest Possible Number questions.

- when asked to add a term to or subtract a term from an average, always return to the sum of the original terms.

- it pays to watch the language in percent word problems so that you accurately identify the percent, part, and whole.

- you need not get thrown by percents less than 1 or greater than 100 – just follow the rules you always use to solve percents questions.

- the first step in a sequence question is to figure out what the pattern is.

- if you can't work backwards on a consecutive integers problem, you can use the facts about averages of groups of consecutive integers to help you solve.

Answer Key

1. E
2. 51
3. B
4. D
5. C
6. D
7. D
8. A
9. D
10. 12

Note: Photocopying any part of this book is prohibited by law.

292

Session 9: Algebra Strategy

In this unit, you will learn to:

- use combination to solve problems with two unknowns.

- work with unusual symbols.

- answer problems involving exponential growth.

Solving for Two Unknowns with the Combination Method

Some equations can be added or subtracted so that one variable is canceled out. This leaves you with an equation you can solve for the other variable.

Look at the following equations:

$$3x + y = 27$$
$$x + y = 15$$

What happens if you subtract the second equation from the first?

$$3x + y = 27$$
$$- (x + y = 15)$$

What is the value of x?

What is the value of y? How did you find it?

What do you notice about the coefficients of the variables that cancelled out?

_____

How can you tell whether to add or subtract one equation from the other?

_____

To Add or to Subtract?

Decide whether each of the following pairs of equations should be added or subtracted to cancel out one variable. Circle the plus sign if you should add them and the minus sign if you should subtract one from the other.

$3x + 3y = 3$ and $3x + y = -2$ $+$ $-$

$2x - y = 2$ and $x + y = 2$ $+$ $-$

$3x + 2x = 7$ and $x - 2x = -3$ $+$ $-$

$5y - x = 1$ and $y - x = -3$ $+$ $-$

$2y + x = 7$ and $-2y + 3x = 0$ $+$ $-$

Combining to Find an Expression with Both Variables

Some questions ask for the value of an expression containing both variables, instead of their individual values. This is a sign that you might be able to combine the equations to end up with this expression (or some multiple of it).

Look at the two equations below. How can you use the combination method to find the value of $x + y$?

$$x + 4y = 9$$
$$5x + 2y = 15$$

Should you add or subtract the equations?

What else do you have to do?

Note: Photocopying any part of this book is prohibited by law.

296

Combination Method: Practice Questions

1. If $8x - y = 32$ and $3x + y = 23$, what is the value of y?

(A) -10
(B) $\dfrac{9}{5}$
(C) 5
(D) 8
(E) 11

2. If $5x + y = 3$ and $4x + 3y = -9$, what is the value of $x - 2y$?

(A) -12
(B) -6
(C) 3
(D) 6
(E) 12

Symbolism Questions

You may come across questions containing unusual symbols or terms, but rest assured that these questions will always define the symbol or term for you. All you have to do is follow the directions. In fact, symbolism questions tend to be easier than other SAT questions, since many of them simply involve plugging into a math formula.

Pretty soon you'll be all smiles when you see symbolism questions.

Symbolism Practice Questions:

3. For all whole numbers n, let $n \blacklozenge = \dfrac{(n-3)^2}{2}$. What is the value $7 \blacklozenge$?

(A) 2
(B) 4
(C) 5
(D) 8
(E) 20

4. For every whole number x, $^\wedge x^\wedge$ is defined as the sum of all the positive factors of x. Which of the following is equal to $^\wedge 10^\wedge$?

(A) $^\wedge 9^\wedge$
(B) $^\wedge 12^\wedge$
(C) $^\wedge 17^\wedge$
(D) $^\wedge 18^\wedge$
(E) $^\wedge 19^\wedge$

Note: Photocopying any part of this book is prohibited by law.

298

Exponential Growth

Exponential growth is defined by an equation that includes a variable exponent, such as:

$$y = 2^x$$

It occurs when a quantity regularly increases by a fixed percentage. For example, a culture of bacteria that triples every 15 minutes is said to increase exponentially.

Can you think of other examples?

While there is an algebraic way to solve, backsolving is a great strategy to use for these questions.

5. The current population of a country is 8 million. Its future population can be expressed as $8{,}000{,}000 \times 2^{\frac{n}{20}}$, where n is the number of years from now. In how many years will the population be 64 million?

(A) 20
(B) 60
(C) 64
(D) 80
(E) 84

Summary

In this unit, you learned that:

- when it's possible, combining equations is the easiest way to solve for two unknowns.

- sometimes you can combine equations to solve for an expression containing both variables.

- when you see an unusual symbol, just follow the directions that go with it.

- backsolving is often the best way to solve an exponential growth question.

Answer Key

1. D
2. E
3. D
4. C
5. B

Session 9: 5-Step Method for Essays

In this unit, you will learn to:

- use Peterson's 5-Step Method for essay writing.

- digest essay prompts.

- brainstorm ideas.

- plan your essay.

- proofread your essay.

Why Do You Need a Method?

You've been writing essays in school for quite a few years, so why do you need a method for the SAT essay?

Think about other things you do in a step-by-step process.

For example:

- You solve algebra problems step-by-step.
- You follow a cooking recipe step-by-step.
- You use instructions to assemble a toy or piece of furniture step-by-step.

Following a method makes it easier to effectively accomplish each of these tasks. The same holds true for using a method to write your SAT essay.

Your Turn

What are the advantages of using a method to write the SAT essay?

_____

_____

_____

_____

Note: Photocopying any part of this book is prohibited by law.

302

Peterson's 5-Step Method for Writing Essays

Step 1: Digest the Prompt (about 2 minutes)

- Make sure you completely understand the question in the assignment.
- Memorize the directions for writing the essay.
- Refer to the quotation or quotations as a possible source for ideas.

Step 2: Brainstorm Ideas (about 2 minutes)

- Write down anything that comes into your head.
- Don't think about what you've written until you've finished brainstorming.
- Write quickly, not worrying about neatness.

Step 3: Plan Your Essay (about 2 minutes)

- Make a rough list, outline, or web to organize your ideas.
- Make sure you can provide supporting details for every idea.
- Think about how each idea connects with your other ideas.

Step 4: Write Your Essay (about 17 minutes)

- Establish your position on the issue early on.
- Use transitions.
- Develop your ideas but avoid needless wordiness and repetition.
- Write a strong conclusion.
- Write neatly!

Step 5: Proofread (about 2 minutes)

- Read each sentence to yourself, making sure it sounds right.
- Check that each sentence uses the appropriate punctuation.
- Make corrections as neatly as possible in the answer booklet.

Step 1: Digest the Prompt

Here's a typical prompt, much like the one you will see on Test Day.

Directions: Think carefully about the issue presented in the quote below and the assignment that follows it.

When you're finally up on the moon, looking back at the earth, all these differences and nationalistic traits are pretty well going to blend and you're going to get a concept that maybe this is really one world and why can't we learn to live together like decent people?
Frank Borman, NASA astronaut

Assignment: What is your view on the idea that differences between cultures and nations are not as great as they seem? Plan and write an essay developing your point of view. Support your position with reasoning and examples taken from your reading, studies, experience, or observations.

To digest the prompt:

- quickly read the quotation or quotations at the beginning of the prompt.
- focus on the question posed in the assignment.
- put the question in your own words to make sure you understand it.
- scan the instructions given after the question. These will always be similar, so don't spend more than a few seconds here.
- go back to the quotation(s) and look for specific ideas you can use or develop in your essay.

Put the question in your own words:

_____

_____

Note: Photocopying any part of this book is prohibited by law.

304

Step 2: Brainstorm Ideas

Think about the prompt you just read. Here are the types of ideas to brainstorm.

General Ideas

Your general ideas are what you think about the differences between cultures and why. Brainstorm some examples now:

_____

What You've Experienced

Your life experiences are your most important source for examples. Think about experiences you've had that introduced you to different cultures:

_____

What You've Observed

You can write about other people's experiences too. Have you observed something in a friend or relative's life that is relevant to the issue?

_____

What You've Read

Use ideas from books and stories you've read. Anything that you think addresses the essay prompt is fair game—just avoid plot summary.

_____

What You've Studied

Draw on your years of schooling. What have you learned in school that might apply here?

_____

Note: Photocopying any part of this book is prohibited by law.

305

Step 3: Plan Your Essay

You won't have time to rewrite your essay, so you need a plan before you write even the first sentence. Here are a few ways you can organize your thoughts.

Make a List

The simplest way to organize your ideas is to mark up your brainstorming list. This method is quick and easy, but it won't help you add specific examples and details to the ideas you already have. Use the list method if you've brainstormed several usable reasons and details.

Make an Outline

The outline is the usual method for organizing ideas. Using Roman numerals, list your thesis, reasons and support, and conclusion in order.

You can use this template:

I.   Thesis

II.   Reason/Example 1
      - Support 1
      - Support 2
      - Support 3

III. Reason/Example 2
      - Support 1
      - Support 2
      - Support 3

IV.   Conclusion

Step 3: Plan Your Essay (continued)

Make a Web

A web is simply an outline that you draw.

Yours might look like this:

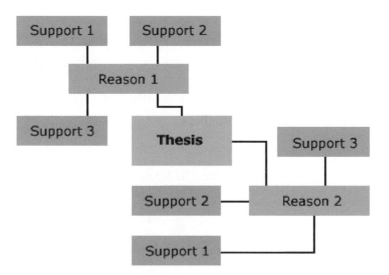

Your Turn

Take your ideas from the brainstorming exercise and make either an outline or a web with them in the space below.

Note: Photocopying any part of this book is prohibited by law.

307

Steps 1-3

You may be tempted to rush through the first three steps, but that would be a mistake. Each step is vital to crafting an essay that earns a 4 or higher.

Get some more practice with Steps 1, 2, and 3 with the new writing prompt below.

Step 1: Digest the prompt

Directions: Think carefully about the issue presented in the quotes below and the assignment that follows it.

There are always flowers for those who want to see them.
Henri Matisse

The man who is a pessimist before 48 knows too much; if he is an optimist after it, he knows too little.
Mark Twain

Assignment: What is your opinion about the role that attitude plays in an individual's life experiences? How does an optimistic or pessimistic attitude affect an individual? Plan and write an essay explaining your position, using reasoning and examples from your studies, experiences, or observations.

Now that you've worked with the prompt, move on to Steps 2 and 3. Don't brainstorm for much more than two minutes before going to Step 3.

Step 2: Brainstorm Ideas

Step 3: Plan Your Essay

Step 4: Write Your Essay

Now it's time to write your essay. You've organized your ideas, so now you just need to express them in sentences and paragraphs.

Here are a few things to keep in mind:

- Don't change your mind. Add details and examples, but stick to your position on the issue and general plan.

- Develop and support the ideas you included in your plan.

- Use transitions when you shift from one idea or paragraph to the next.

- Write as carefully and neatly as possible. Make the indent of each new paragraph clear. Leave enough space in the margins to allow for last-minute corrections.

- Keep your eye on the clock, and give yourself enough time to write a conclusion. Not writing a conclusion will hurt your score.

Write the opening paragraph to the essay you just planned:

_____

_____

_____

_____

_____

_____

Step 5: Proofread Your Work

Errors are bound to crop up in an essay when you are concentrating on writing for content. That's why you must devote your final two minutes to proofreading.

Your Turn

Read through this student essay and see how many errors you can spot.

I am proud to live in country and in a state, Texas that contains citizens of diverse cultural backgrounds who live together in peace. When I study current events and history reading how ethnic rivalries are often at the root of so many wars, I wonder how we do it. Perhaps it's because we live in a nation of immigrants from all over the world that we realize that how we are similiar is so much more important than how we are different. This makes ours a very fortunate soceity. Through my experiences with an emmigrant family, I have found that under surface differences, we all believe and want most of the same things.

One of my best friends Dima Sudzukovic comes from the former Yugoslavia. He and his parents emigrated to the United States back several years ago when civil war gripped his country. According to Dima, the language and cultural differences between the various ethnic groups in the former Yugoslavia was actually very small, but these differences became exaggerated after the fall of communism when people rediscovered grievances against one another and every ethnic group tried to form their own state. Dima is very grateful to be living in a country that embraces so many ethnicities and religious groups, focusing on the many things people have in common instead of the few differences.

Although Dima has become very American since moving to Texas, but I have met his parents who are still very "old world" including often speaking in their native language. At first they seemed radically different than most parents I now, including my own. For one thing they are very bookish and while they except their children to be respectful they also seem to relish debating "big ideas" with anyone who care to argue with them. Their habits and discussions may not be what I'm used to, but just like any other parents they want the very best for their children and are willing to work and sacrifice to make that happen.

Getting to know the Sudzukovic family has taught me to respect many things about my country, it's general tolerance towards immigrants and different ethnic group. I've come to see that people are more alike than we sometimes care to admit. It may sound like a naïve statement, but people everywhere should appreciate each others similarities and differences. Their what makes the world an interesting place.

Summary

In this unit, you learned that:

- the first step in writing the SAT essay is to make sure you understand the essay prompt.

- you can brainstorm ideas from your life, observations, or studies.

- planning with an outline or web will help you write an organized, cohesive essay.

- you should stick to your plan when you write your essay.

- you should always leave a couple of minutes at the end of the essay section to proofread your work.

Session 9: Error Identification Strategy

In this unit, you will learn:

- strategies for the Error Identification section of the SAT.

- common mistakes to look for in Error Identification questions.

Error Identification Overview

In the Error Identification section of the test, you'll see questions that look like this:

Each person at the conference, a gathering of scientists, were required to
  A   B   C

register several months in advance. No error
                      D   E

Your job is to choose which one of the underlined portions, if any, contains an error.

Remember:

- Each sentence contains either one error or no errors.
- No sentence contains more than one error.

Choice (E): No Error

The original sentence won't always have an error—sometimes the correct answer is choice (E), No error. Expect that choice (E) will be the correct answer to at least one Error Identification question. However, don't get lazy and blindly select choice (E); for the majority of questions, it won't be the correct answer. Before you choose choice (E):

1. Read each underlined section carefully, looking for common mistakes.

2. Think about whether any underlined piece looks like it could possibly be wrong, even if you're not sure.

3. Remember that it's more likely for a sentence to contain an error than not.

4. Remember that some of the sentences (possibly several) will not contain an error.

5. Trust your instincts. If a sentence looks correct, pick choice (E).

Note: Photocopying any part of this book is prohibited by law.

314

Solving Error Identification Questions

Solve Error Identification questions by using the 3-step method:

1) **Read the sentence.** As you read, sort each underlined portion into categories: Definitely Correct, Definitely Incorrect, and Not Sure.

2) **Pick your answer.** Optimally, you'll find only one Definitely Incorrect portion; if not, move on to step 3.

3) **Reread the sentence.** If you're not sure of the correct answer, or if you think there are no errors, take another look, checking for classic SAT writing errors (you'll learn about these shortly).

Now try solving this Error Identification question using the 3-step method.

<u>Each person</u> at the <u>conference,</u> a gathering of scientists, <u>were required</u> to
   A   B   C

register several months <u>in advance</u>. <u>No error</u>
                        D   E

Does anything jump out at you as being Definitely Incorrect? How about Definitely Correct?

Common Error Identification Mistakes

Subject/Verb Agreement

What is the verb in the following sentence? Does it match the subject?

> Each athlete, after the games are over, participate in an awards ceremony.

Parallelism

Which verb in the sentence below is unlike the others?

> The campers enjoyed many activities, including swimming, hiking, and to play baseball.

What are the pronouns in this next sentence? Do they match?

> Whether or not you believe her story, one has to admit that she tells it well.

Comparisons

What comparison is made in the sentence below? What comparison should be made?

> Unlike the director's first movie, people flocked to see the second.

Verb Tense

You might not catch a verb tense error just by glancing at the underlined piece. You'll need to consider it in the context of the sentence as a whole. Which verb below does not match the rest of the sentence?

> The tornado, which could has done a great deal of damage, did not harm any of the houses in our neighborhood.

Pronouns

When you see an underlined pronoun, look carefully not just at the pronoun itself, but also at the noun it replaces. What is the pronoun in the sentence below? What word does it replace? Is it correct?

> Andrew owned a saxophone, which he had received for one of his birthdays, but he had never learned to play them.

Adjectives and Adverbs

When you see an underlined adjective or adverb, quickly check to see what word it describes. What adjective appears in the sentence below, and what does it describe? Is it correct?

> No matter how careful they planned their trip, they always got lost.

Practice Questions

Use the concepts you've learned so far to solve these practice questions. Remember to look out for common errors.

1. <u>An inventor</u> need not be <u>brilliant,</u> but he or she must have <u>patience,</u>
      A   B   C

   perseverance, and the ability to solve problems using <u>unconventional methods</u>.
                                                           D

   <u>No error</u>
      E

2. We knew that <u>crucial to our</u> plans <u>were</u> the participation <u>of the entire</u>
                     A   B   C

   <u>group</u>. <u>No error</u>
     D   E

3. If you look at the night sky, <u>one</u> can sometimes <u>see</u> the planet Venus
                                  A   B

   <u>as well as</u> several <u>constellations</u>. <u>No error</u>
      C   D   E

4. Of the <u>two experiments</u>, the second was <u>the least</u> helpful in showing the
             A   B

   <u>harmful effects</u> of pollution on crops and in <u>suggesting</u> healthier alternatives.
      C   D

   <u>No error</u>
      E

5. Just like the paid staff, the <u>volunteers at</u> the community center <u>work</u> hard,
                            A   B

   cleaning, painting, and generally <u>they do</u> whatever chores need to be done.
      C   D

   <u>No error</u>
      E

6. <u>Unlike other</u> big <u>cats</u>, such as <u>the lion and the tiger</u>, <u>the claws of the cheetah</u>
     A   B   C   D

are not fully retractable. <u>No error</u>
                      E

7. The current drought, <u>which had</u> severely <u>compromised</u> the region's crops,
                    A   B

<u>will have lasted</u> for seven <u>months by</u> the end of July. <u>No error</u>
    C   D   E

8. <u>Each speaker</u> had the chance to express <u>his or her</u> opinion about the
      A   B

<u>new policy</u> changes, <u>which had gone</u> into effect the previous month. <u>No error</u>
   C   D   E

9. The fiction of Gabriel García Márquez, <u>which takes</u> readers to a world that is
                                  A

richly described but not <u>quite possible</u>, is <u>very different from authors</u> who write in
                   B   C

a <u>strictly realistic</u> style. <u>No error</u>
   D   E

10. <u>After years</u> of research, the <u>team of scientists</u> decided that, <u>having only began</u>
     A   B   C

to scratch the surface of the problem, <u>it</u> needed to secure new funding for the
                                D

next phase of the project. <u>No error</u>
                     E

Summary

In this unit, you learned that:

- you should solve Error Identification questions using the 3-step method.

- common errors include mistakes in subject-verb agreement, parallelism, comparisons, verb tense, pronouns, and adjectives and adverbs.

Answer Key

1. E
2. B
3. A
4. B
5. D
6. D
7. A
8. E
9. C
10. C

Session 10: Coordinate Geometry

In this unit, you will learn to:

- identify a point on the coordinate axes from its x- and y-coordinates.

- find the length of a line segment graphed in the coordinate plane.

- find the midpoint of a line segment graphed in the coordinate plane.

- find the slope of a line.

- use the equation of a line to identify its slope, y-intercept, or a point that it includes.

- recognize the relationships between the slopes of parallel and perpendicular lines.

- match an equation to the linear function that represents it and vice versa.

The Coordinate Axes

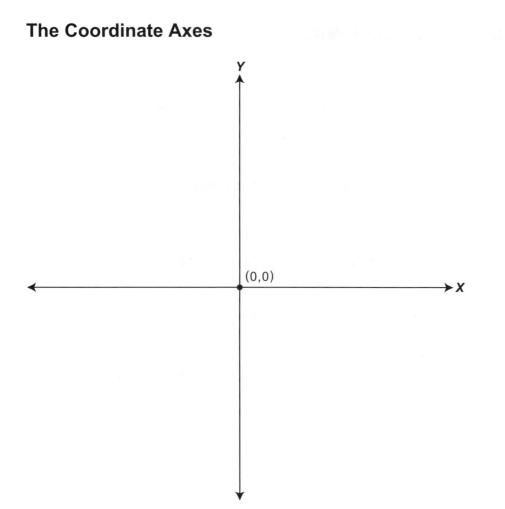

Coordinate geometry questions involve points and line segments graphed on the coordinate axes. Test questions often say that these figures are graphed in the *xy*-plane.

The coordinate axes are made up of a horizontal number line called the *x*-axis, which is crossed at a right angle by a vertical number line called the y-axis.

The point where these axes cross is called the origin and is often labeled as 0.

Plotting Points

To answer coordinate geometry questions, you must understand how the positions of points on the axes are described.

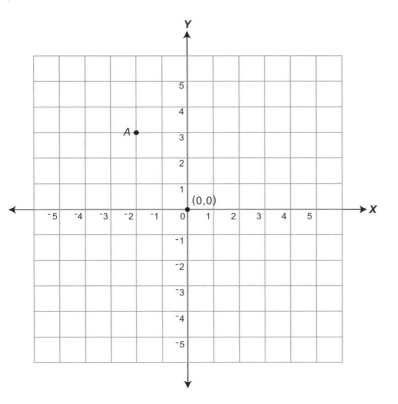

A point on the axes is identified by its *x*-coordinate and *y*-coordinate. The coordinates for a point are written as (*x*, *y*).

The origin has (0, 0) as its coordinates.

The *x*-coordinate tells how far to the right or left of the origin a point is. Points to the right of the origin have positive x-coordinates, and points to the left of it have negative *x*-coordinates.

The *y*-coordinate tells how far above or below the origin a point is. Points above the origin have positive y-coordinates, and points below it have negative *y*-coordinates.

What are the coordinates of point *A* graphed above?

Distance

Some questions ask you to find the lengths of segments graphed on the axes. The length of a segment is the distance between its endpoints.

Determining the Length of a Line Segment from a Graph

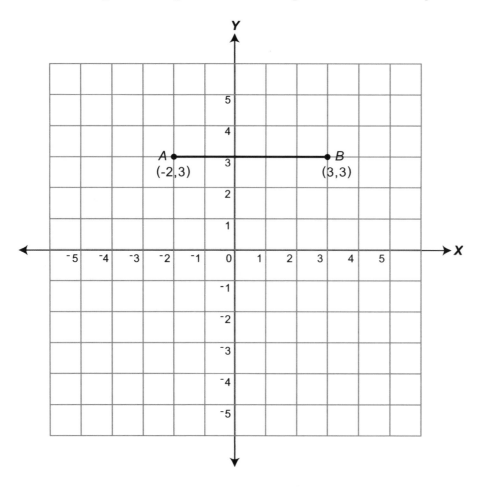

What is the length of line segment $\overline{AB}$?

Remember that **distance is always positive**. Even though part of line segment $\overline{AB}$ is to the left of the origin where x-coordinates are negative, this piece still has a positive length value. A distance of two units to the left is still a distance of 2 units.

Finding the Length of a Line Segment from Its Endpoints

You don't need a graph to find the length of a line segment. The coordinates of its endpoints are all you need to find the length of the segment.

When the endpoints have the same *x*-coordinate, the length of the segment is the difference between its *y*-coordinates.

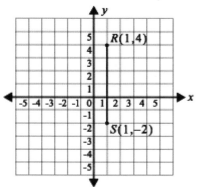

What is the length of segment $\overline{RS}$?

When the endpoints have the same *y*-coordinate, the length of the segment is the difference between its *x*-coordinates.

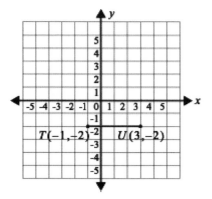

What is the length of segment $\overline{TU}$?

Distance Formula

If the endpoints of a segment don't have a common coordinate, you can use the distance formula to solve for its length.

Find the distance, d, between endpoints (x_1, y_1) and (x_2, y_2) with the formula:

$$d = \sqrt{(x_1 - x_2)^2 + (y_1 - y_2)^2}$$

Plugging into the Formula

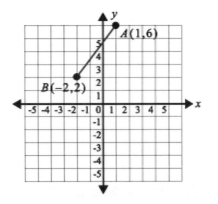

Plug the coordinates into the formula to find the length of $\overline{AB}$.

See the Segment as the Hypotenuse of a Right Triangle

There's another way to find the length of a segment when its endpoints don't have a common coordinate.

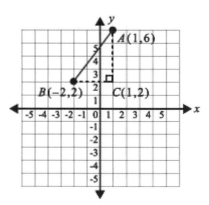

Sketching in $\overline{AC}$ and $\overline{BC}$ produces right triangle ABC. $\overline{AB}$ is its hypotenuse. If you know the lengths of its legs, you can plug their values into the Pythagorean Theorem and solve for the hypotenuse.

Can you find the lengths of $\overline{AC}$ and $\overline{BC}$?

Once you know the length of the two legs, plug them into the Pythagorean Theorem to find the length of $\overline{AB}$.

$$\text{hypotenuse} = \overline{AB} = \sqrt{(\text{leg}_1)^2 + (\text{leg}_2)^2}$$

Elimination Strategies

Once you find the lengths of the legs, you can eliminate answers on a multiple-choice question. It's often possible to narrow it down to two choices.

Suppose that the question asking for the length of $\overline{AB}$ included the following choices:

(A) 3
(B) 4
(C) 5
(D) 6
(E) 7

Using the following facts, decide which answer choices can be eliminated.

- The hypotenuse is the longest side of a right triangle.
Eliminate choices:

- The third side of a triangle must be less than the sum of its two other sides.
Eliminate choices:

Note: Photocopying any part of this book is prohibited by law.

328

Finding Distance: Practice Questions

This question asks you to combine your knowledge of plane geometry with coordinate geometry.

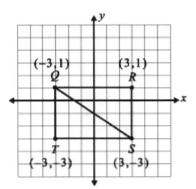

1. Rectangle $QRST$ is graphed in the xy-plane as shown above. What is the area of right triangle QRS in square units?

(A) 4
(B) 6
(C) 9
(D) 12
(E) 24

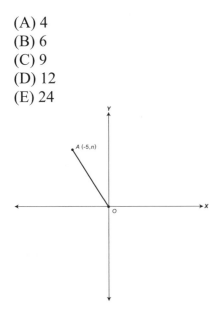

2. In the xy-plane above, $\overline{AO} = 13$. What is the value of n?

(A) – 13
(B) – 12
(C) 5
(D) 8
(E) 12

Midpoint

If you know the endpoints of a line segment, you can find its midpoint. The midpoint is the point that divides a segment into two equal halves (this is also called bisecting).

The coordinates of the midpoint are found using the formula:

$$\left(\frac{x_1 + x_2}{2}, \frac{y_1 + y_2}{2}\right)$$

where (x_1, y_1) and (x_2, y_2) are its endpoints.

To help you remember the formula, think for a minute about what you're doing. You're averaging the coordinates of the endpoints.

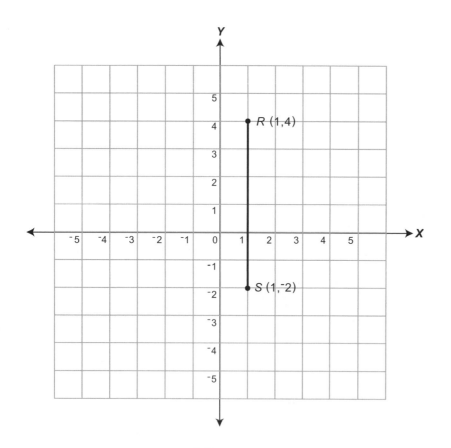

What is the midpoint of $\overline{RS}$?

Note: Photocopying any part of this book is prohibited by law.

330

Midpoint: Practice Question

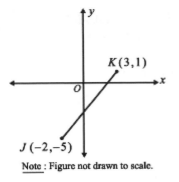

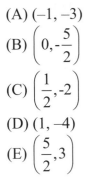

Note : Figure not drawn to scale.

3. What are the coordinates of the midpoint of $\overline{JK}$?

(A) $(-1, -3)$

(B) $\left(0, -\dfrac{5}{2}\right)$

(C) $\left(\dfrac{1}{2}, -2\right)$

(D) $(1, -4)$

(E) $\left(\dfrac{5}{2}, 3\right)$

Slope

The slope of a line is also called its rise over its run and is basically a measure of how steep it is. It is the vertical change of the line divided by its horizontal change.

If you know two points on a line, you can find its slope using the formula:

$$m = \frac{y_2 - y_1}{x_2 - x_1}$$

where m is the slope and (x_1, y_1) and (x_2, y_2) are two points on the line.

You can use any two points on a line to plug into the formula; the slope will always be the same. It also doesn't matter which point you call (x_1, y_1) and which (x_2, y_2). The slope is the same either way.

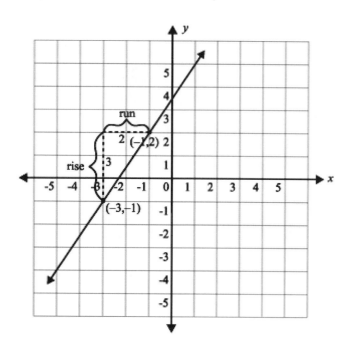

What is the slope of this line?

Note: Photocopying any part of this book is prohibited by law.

332

Counting Off

You can also "count off" to find the slope of a line.

Think of slope as the number of units you must move up or down to get from one point to the next, divided by the number of units you need to move right or left to get from one point to the next.

Moving up and to the right are positive changes; moving down and to the left are negative changes.

Starting at point (−3, −1), you need to move 3 units up and 2 units to the right to get to point (−1, 2), so the slope is _____.

This method can also help you find the coordinates of other points on the line.

Starting at point (−1, 2) count off to find the coordinates of another point on the line:

Note: Photocopying any part of this book is prohibited by law.

333

Positive and Negative Slope

The direction of a line can tell you whether its slope is positive or negative.

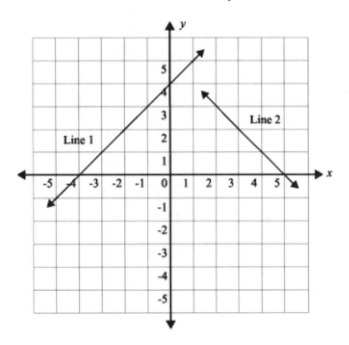

- A line that slants upward from left to right has a positive slope.
- A line that slants downward from left to right has a negative slope.

Line 1 has a _____ slope.

Line 2 has a _____ slope.

Slope: Practice Question

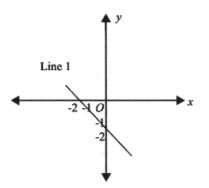

4. What is the slope of line 1 shown in the figure above?

(A) – 2
(B) – 1
(C) $-\dfrac{1}{2}$
(D) 1
(E) 2

Note: Photocopying any part of this book is prohibited by law.

335

Equation of a Line

A line graphed on the coordinate axes can be represented by the equation:

$$y = mx + b$$

Where:

m represents the slope

b represents the *y*-intercept (the *y*-coordinate of the point where the line crosses the *y*-axis)

x and *y* represent the coordinates of any point on the line

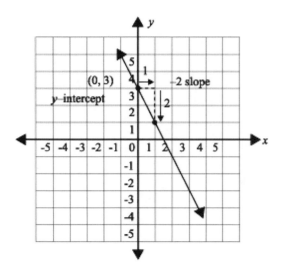

What is the equation of this line?

The coordinates of any point that lies on the line will make the equation true when they are plugged in for *x* and *y*. Check your equation by plugging in the coordinates (1, 1):

Slope-Intercept Form

Remember: you cannot identify m or b until the equation is in slope-intercept form: $y = mx + b$.

This means that y must be alone on one side of the equation with a coefficient of 1.

$$2y + x = 4$$

If you try to identify m and b from the equation above you'll get $m = 1$ and $b = 4$, both of which are incorrect.

First write this equation in slope-intercept form:

Now identify m and b:

Equation of a Line: Practice Question

5. What is the slope of the line identified by $-3y = -2(2x - 1)$?

(A) -4

(B) $-\dfrac{2}{3}$

(C) $\dfrac{3}{4}$

(D) $\dfrac{4}{3}$

(E) 2

Parallel and Perpendicular Lines

If two lines are parallel, their slopes are equal to each other.

If two lines are perpendicular, their slopes are negative reciprocals of each other.

So, if a line has a slope of m:

- any line parallel to it has a slope of m.
- any line perpendicular to it has a slope of $-\dfrac{1}{m}$.

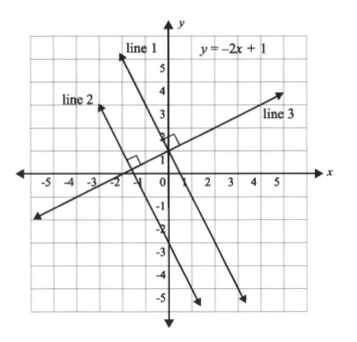

In the figure above, the equation of line 1 is $y = -2x + 1$.

Since line 2 is parallel to line 1, the slope of line 2 is _____.

Since line 3 is perpendicular to line 1, the slope of line 3 is _____.

Note: Since lines 1 and 2 are parallel, and line 3 is perpendicular to line 1, line 2 is also perpendicular to line 3.

Parallel and Perpendicular Lines: Practice Question

6. What is the slope of any line parallel to the line $2y + x = 5$?

(A) -1

(B) $-\dfrac{1}{2}$

(C) 1

(D) $\dfrac{1}{2}$

(E) 2

Working with Graphs

Graphs of lines will appear in some SAT questions. You may be asked to identify a graph given its equation or the equation of a line given its graph.

Use the Slope and *y*-Intercept

- Use equation to ID graph: Identify m and b from the slope-intercept equation and then eliminate graphs that don't match both.

- Use graph to ID equation: Identify the slope and intercept from the graph and then plug them in for *m* and *b* in the equation $y = mx + b$.

Work Backwards

The coordinates of every point on a line will make its equation true when plugged in for *x* and *y*.

- Use equation to ID graph: Use the given equation to test points from the graphs in the choices. Eliminate a graph as soon as its coordinates fail to make the equation true.

- Use graph to ID equation: Test points from the given graph in the equations in the choices. Eliminate an equation as soon as a point fails to make it true.

Tip: When working backwards, use points that are easy to work with, points whose coordinates are zero and small positive integers.

Working with Graphs: Practice Question

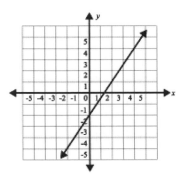

7. Which equation describes the line graphed above?

(A) $y = -2x - 2$

(B) $y = -2x + \dfrac{3}{2}$

(C) $y = \dfrac{3}{2}x - 2$

(D) $y = \dfrac{3}{2}x + \dfrac{3}{2}$

(E) $y = \dfrac{2}{3}x - 2$

Summary

In this unit, you learned that:

- points on the coordinate axes are identified by their *x*- and *y*-coordinates.

- if the endpoints have a common coordinate, the length of the segment is the difference between the different coordinates.

- you can plug the coordinates of the endpoints of a line segment into the distance formula to solve for its length.

- you can treat the segment as the hypotenuse of a right triangle and draw in its legs to find its length.

- the midpoint of a segment can be found using the formula: midpoint = $\left(\dfrac{x_1 + x_2}{2}, \dfrac{y_1 + y_2}{2} \right)$, which is basically averaging the coordinates of its endpoints.

- the slope of a line is a measure of its steepness, and can be found using the formula $m = \dfrac{y_2 - y_1}{x_2 - x_1}$ where (x_1, y_1) and (x_2, y_2) are two points on the line.

- since the slope of a line is its rise over its run, you can find the slope by counting off the number of units you need to go up and over from one point on the line to the next.

- the slope-intercept equation of a line is $y = mx + b$, where *m* is the slope, *b* is the *y*-intercept, and *x* and *y* stand for the coordinates of any point on the line.

- if the coordinates of a point satisfy the equation of a line, that point lies on the line.

- the slopes of parallel lines are equal; the slopes of perpendicular lines are negative reciprocals.

- the slope and *y*-intercept of a line can help identify its graph on the *xy*-plane.

Answer Key

1. D
2. E
3. C
4. B
5. D
6. B
7. C

Session 10: Functions

In this unit, you will learn to:

- recognize and evaluate functions.

- evaluate a function.

- understand the concepts of domain and range.

- determine the values for which a function does not exist.

- work with direct and inverse relations.

Understanding Functions

A function is an equation that describes the relationship between two variables.

Look at this equation:

$$y = 2x$$

This equation shows that for each value of x, the value of y is twice the value of x.

The above can also be written in function notation, with f(x) replacing the variable y:

$$f(x) = 2x$$

This is read as "*f* of *x* equals 2*x*."

The two equations mean the same thing, but the second highlights the fact that the value of the function depends on the value of *x*.

Functions in the Real World

Functional relationships exist in the real world—for example, paychecks. If your hourly wage is $10, the amount of your paycheck is a function of the number of hours you work. If you let x be the number of hours you work and y be the dollar amount of your paycheck, you can show the relationship between the hours you work and how much you are paid like this:

$$y = 10x$$

In function notation you could write this as:

$$f(x) = 10x$$

Try to think of some other examples of functional relationships, and write them using function notation:

Evaluating Functions

You evaluate a function by finding the function's value for a given x. In other words, you find the value of $f(x)$ for a given x by plugging that x into the equation.

Look at the function $f(x) = 2x$ again. When x equals 5, the value of f(x) is:

$$f(5) = 2(5) = 10$$

Think about the paycheck function. How much would you earn if you worked 5 hours?

Functions on the SAT will be a little more complicated than these examples.

Try this one:

If $f(x) = \dfrac{x-3}{4}$, what is $f(15) + f(19)$?

Evaluating Functions: Practice Question

1. For $f(x) = x^2 + 2x + k$, the value of $f(3)$ is 10. What is the value of k?

(A) –5
(B) –3
(C) 7
(D) 15
(E) 120

Domain and Range

The domain of a function is the set of all "input" values for which the function is defined.

What's the domain of $f(x) = x^2$?

When $f(x) = x^2$, you can plug in any real number for x and get a real number value for $f(x)$. So the domain of this function is the set of all real numbers.

The range of a function is the set of all possible "output" values of the function.

What's the range of $f(x) = x^2$?

When $f(x) = x^2$, no matter what number you plug in for x, $f(x)$ is not negative. This is because the square of a negative number is always positive. So the range of this function is the set of all nonnegative numbers.

Note: Photocopying any part of this book is prohibited by law.

349

Values for Which a Function Does Not Exist

For most functions, x can be any real number value; but for some, there are values of x for which the function does not exist. When you see certain kinds of functions, you need to think about what values of x are impossible.

Functions with x in the Denominator

Remember that a fraction with a denominator of 0 is not defined. If a function has an x in the denominator, the range is all real numbers except values of x that make the denominator 0:

The domain of the function $f(x) = \dfrac{1}{x^2 - 16}$ is all real numbers EXCEPT _____ and _____.

Functions with x in a Square Root Sign

The square root of a negative number is an imaginary number, not a real number. If a function has an x under a square root sign, the domain is all real numbers except those values of x that make the quantity inside the square root sign negative.

The domain of the function $f(x) = \sqrt{x + 7}$ is all real numbers EXCEPT _____.

This can also be written as the inequality _____.

Domain and Range: Practice Questions

2. For which values of x is the function $f(x) = \dfrac{2-x}{x^2 + 3x - 10}$ undefined?

(A) 0
(B) 2
(C) 3 and −10
(D) −5 and 2
(E) −2 and 5

3. What is the domain of the function $f(x) = \dfrac{1}{3} + \sqrt{16 - 2x}$?

(A) All real numbers greater than 16
(B) All real numbers less than 16
(C) All real numbers greater than 8
(D) All real numbers less than 8
(E) All real numbers less than or equal to 8

Direct Variation

Two variables vary directly if multiplying one variable by a factor results in the multiplication of the other variable by that same factor. Functions with direct variation look like this:

$$y = kx \qquad \text{or} \qquad f(x) = kx$$

where k is a constant.

Think back to the function example with a paycheck, earning $10 for each hour worked. The amount of the paycheck varies directly with the number of hours you work. If you work one hour, you earn $10. If you work 5 times as many hours (5 hours), you earn 5 times as much money ($50).

Again, this function is written as $y = 10x$ or $f(x) = 10x$.

Basically, in a direct variation, when one variable increases so does the other; when one variable decreases so does the other. Remembering this fact can help you eliminate some answer choices.

Direct Variation: Practice Question

4. If x varies directly as y, and $x = 30$ when $y = 10$, which of the following equals x when $y = 17$?

(A) 3
(B) 10
(C) 23
(D) 34
(E) 51

Indirect Variation

Two variables vary inversely if multiplying one variable by a factor results in the multiplication of the other variable by the reciprocal of that factor. Functions with inverse variation look like this:

$$y = \frac{k}{x} \qquad \text{or} \qquad f(x) = \frac{k}{x}$$

where k is a constant.

A real-world inverse relationship is the relationship between time and speed when traveling a certain distance. The slower the speed, the more time spent traveling and vice versa. This relationship is summarized by the rate formula:

$$\text{Rate} = \frac{\text{Distance}}{\text{Time}}$$

Traveling 100 miles at a rate of 50 mph takes 2 hours. If the speed were reduced by half, the number of hours spent traveling would have to double for the equality to be maintained:

$$50 \text{mph} = \frac{100 \text{ miles}}{2 \text{ hours}} \qquad 25 \text{ mph} = \frac{100 \text{ miles}}{4 \text{ hours}}$$

Basically, in an indirect variation, when one variable increases, the other decreases and vice versa. Remembering this fact can help you eliminate some answer choices.

Indirect Variation: Practice Question

5. If x varies inversely as y, and $x = 6$ when $y = 8$, which of the following is the value of x when $y = 12$?

(A) 4
(B) 6
(C) 8
(D) 9
(E) 12

Summary

In this unit, you learned that:

- a function is a relationship between two variables in which the value of one variable depends on the value of the other.

- to evaluate a function for a certain value of x, plug in the given value for x.

- the domain of a function is the set of input values for which the function is defined, and the range of a function is the set of output values.

- there may be values for which a function is undefined. Beware of such exceptions when you see an x in the denominator or under a radical sign in a function.

- in direct relationships, variables move in the same direction.

- in inverse relationships, variables move in opposite directions.

Answer Key

1. A
2. D
3. E
4. E
5. A

Note: Photocopying any part of this book is prohibited by law.

354

Session 10: Organization and Style in Essays

In this unit, you will learn to:

- use the Standard Essay Template to write an effective SAT essay.

- identify strong introductions, supporting details, transitions, and conclusions.

- select signal words for different essay uses.

- write a thesis statement and topic sentences.

- use the principles of style to make your essay stand out from the pack.

- avoid some of the most common writing errors.

The Standard Essay Template

To write a successful essay, you must develop and organize your ideas. To help you do that, we created a Standard Essay Template.

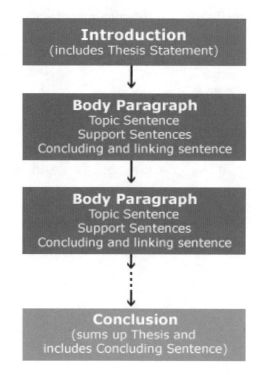

Introduction:

_____

_____

Body paragraphs:

_____

_____

Conclusion:

_____

_____

Introductions

A good introduction should:

- answer the question from the writing assignment.
- provide an effective lead-in to the body of the essay.

Your Turn

Complete the introduction of an essay written based on the assignment below.

"What is your view on the idea that it is more important to be true to yourself than to conform to the expectations of others? Plan and write an essay developing your point of view."

The history of America is rich with examples of people who were true to their own convictions instead of behaving like everyone else. Many of these people actually changed society for the better. Henry David Thoreau was one such person, and a more modern example is former Illinois governor George Ryan. _____

_____

_____

_____

_____

Note: Photocopying any part of this book is prohibited by law.

357

Topic Sentences

A strong SAT essay presents the main idea of each body paragraph in a topic sentence. While the thesis statement introduces the author's position, and the concluding sentence sums it up, topic sentences present the main point of each body paragraph.

Your Turn

Write a topic sentence for each body paragraph below.

_____

_____

In the years leading up to the Civil War, Thoreau was a vocal opponent against slavery. To protest slavery and the government that allowed it, Thoreau refused to pay his federal taxes. For this refusal, Thoreau was thrown in jail. While there, he wrote an essay called "Civil Disobedience," encouraging people to stand up for their beliefs and break laws that were unjust. His essay influenced generations of leaders. For example, during the Civil Rights Movement of the 1960s, Dr. Martin Luther King, Jr. drew on Thoreau's ideas to lead nonviolent protests that eventually changed unfair laws.

_____

_____

While Ryan was governor, evidence came out proving that an Illinois man who had been convicted of a crime and sentenced to death wasn't actually guilty of the crime. Soon after, another convict on death row was proved not guilty through new evidence. Eventually, Governor Ryan called a halt to all executions in the state, saying that there was obviously a problem with the system. Then Governor Ryan made a very unpopular move—he commuted all of the death row sentences in Illinois. He believed the system was so flawed that this was necessary. Through his actions, Governor Ryan opened a national discussion about capital punishment that will likely lead to reforms in the system.

Developing Ideas

A good writer goes beyond merely stating ideas; a good writer develops ideas with effective supporting details.

Your Turn

Supply supporting details for the body paragraph below.

Following laws is one way that it is necessary for people to conform to the expectations of others. For example, a simple drive across town would be chaotic and dangerous if other drivers didn't do what is expected of them.

_____

_____

_____

_____

_____

_____

_____

Transitions

A good essay smoothly transitions from one idea to another, and in particular from one paragraph to another. Here are some signal words to use in your essay.

Give an example.	• For example • For instance • In fact
Add a thought.	• In addition • Also • Furthermore • What's more
Indicate cause and effect.	• Because • Therefore • Thus • As a result
Emphasize a thought.	• Indeed • In fact • Clearly • Most importantly
Compare and contrast.	Comparison: • Similarly • Just as ... so • Like, likewise Contrast: • On the other hand • But • Although, though, even though • However
Show chronological order.	• Then • Next • Finally • Before • After, afterwards
Conclude.	• To sum up • In summary • To summarize • In conclusion

Using Transitions

Your Turn

Fill in the missing signal words in the student essay below. You can use the transitions listed on the previous page, or you can come up with some of your own.

In life, there are many pressures to conform to the standards and expectations that others have set for us. Sometimes it's just prudent and wise to "go with the flow" and not resist these pressures too strongly. _____ there are times when we must fight back, taking a difficult or unpopular stand in order to be true to ourselves.

_____ of this is the story of Celie in Alice Walker's novel The Color Purple. From her earliest memories, almost everyone in Celie's life treats her as though she were stupid, useless, and ugly. When she is forced into marrying a man she doesn't love, she initially accepts his degrading treatment of her. _____, she lets herself believe that she is worthless. _____, through the friendship of another woman, Celie _____ learns to stand up for herself and exceed the limited expectations that others have set for her. She fights what e. e. cummings refers to as "the hardest battle any human being can fight" and eventually succeeds in building her own family, business, and happiness.

_____ literary example is Fanny in Jane Austen's Mansfield Park. Fanny lives with her aunt and uncle, who are much wealthier than her own parents. Fanny's cousins take advantage of the luxuries their parents can afford, and they often abuse their privileges. _____ Fanny feels like an outsider, she does not alter who she is in order to fit in with her adopted family. _____, Fanny remains true to her upbringing and morals and doesn't fall into the decadent lifestyle that ruins her cousins.

If we don't listen to our inner voices, if we never resist the pressures to conform to the expectations of others, then we eventually lose the ability to think and act for ourselves. _____, we never discover our own potential for greatness.

Note: Photocopying any part of this book is prohibited by law.

361

Conclusions

A good conclusion should do the following:

- sum up and restate the essay's thesis.
- end on a strong note.

A good conclusion often takes the thesis and attempts to push it further by adding a strong closing.

Your Turn

Look at the conclusion to the first sample essay.

Henry David Thoreau and George Ryan are just two examples from countless Americans who have made a difference by sticking to their own beliefs. After all, individuals who followed their own convictions built America. If the Founding Fathers hadn't been willing to stand up for their beliefs and fight for independence from England, we might not have become a country at all.

How does the writer "go beyond" in the final paragraph?

_____

_____

Note: Photocopying any part of this book is prohibited by law.

362

Essay Writing: Step-by-Step

You've seen an essay that follows the template, so now it's your turn to try it on your own.

A new essay prompt is given below. Take five minutes to follow the first three Steps of Peterson's 5-Step Method:

1. Digest the prompt.
2. Brainstorm ideas.
3. Plan your essay.

Then we'll move on to Step 4—writing the essay—together.

Step 1: Digest the Prompt

Directions: Think carefully about the issue presented in the following quote and the assignment below.

First I saw the mountains in the painting; then I saw the painting in the mountains.
--Chinese Proverb

Assignment: What is your view on the idea that art, rather than being a reflection of the world, can help us see the real world in new ways? Plan and write an essay in which you develop your point of view on this issue. Support your position with reasoning and examples taken from your reading, studies, experience, or observations.

Step 2: Brainstorm Ideas

Use this space to brainstorm your ideas.

Step 3: Plan Your Essay

Use this space to plan your essay.

Step 4: Write your Essay

Instead of writing a complete essay now, follow the template and write the sentences that guide the readers through your essay—the thesis statement and the topic sentence of each paragraph you planned.

Thesis Statement:

_____

_____

Topic Sentence, Body Paragraph 1

_____

_____

Topic Sentence, Body Paragraph 2

_____

_____

Note: Photocopying any part of this book is prohibited by law.

365

What Is Style?

Style, in its broadest definition, includes everything about the way writers present themselves in words. This includes the words they choose, the types of sentences they use, and the variety of sentences they use.

1. What are some examples of writing that have an informal style?

_____

_____

2. What are some examples of writing that have a formal style?

_____

_____

3. What kind of style should you use in your SAT essay?

_____

_____

Be Concise

There are three principles of SAT essay style—be concise, be forceful, and be creative.

Being concise means getting your point across as directly as possible.

Your Turn

4. Rewrite the following sentence to make it more concise.

> In spite of the fact that I have only a little bit of experience as a photographer up to this point, I will probably do well with photography in the future because I have a lot of motivation to succeed in this particular pursuit.

_____

_____

_____

Eliminate Redundancies

To be concise in your writing, avoid redundant language. A _redundancy_ is a needlessly repetitive use of words.

Your Turn

5. Read the passage below, underlining any redundancies.

> I currently work as a crime reporter for a major daily newspaper. I have no plans for the future to quit my job, although the work can be depressing, such as when I have to write about some poor indigent who was senselessly strangled to death for no apparent reason. However, one of the last cases that I worked on really made me think to myself that someday I might just walk off the job without giving advance notice.
>
> I was talking to one of the homicide detectives who specializes in crimes of murder. I'm often in contact with police officers in my search for new developments in the latest grisly investigation. I asked him if there were any new leads that might possibly direct the detectives to the murderer who perpetrated the killing. The detective just shrugged his shoulders…

Be Forceful

Good SAT essay writing is active and takes a stand. To make your writing more forceful, avoid the passive voice, wishy-washy statements, and vague language.

6. Rewrite the following sentence to make it more forceful.

> Although I am no expert, I do not think that a satisfactory explanation of our fiscal policy has been provided by our mayor as of yet.

_____

_____

Avoid Needless Qualification

7. Which filler words should be cut from the following sentences?

> The ending of the book was just tragic, if you know what I mean.

> Well, I was actually pretty surprised when I walked in and saw all of my friends.

Use the Active Voice

8. Rewrite the following sentences to eliminate the passive voice.

> The essays are written by students.

_____

> The meals on the cruise were prepared by a world-class chef.

_____

Be Creative

Creativity in writing can mean many things, including varying word choice and creating images.

Vary Word Choice

9. How could you vary the word choice in the sentence below?

> A lot of my friends agree that I use a lot of the same words over and over again. It used to bother me a lot, but now I try not to think a lot about it.

_____

_____

Create Images

10. Rewrite the following sentence using imagery.

> After a day of skiing, we were all tired.

_____

_____

Write In Complete Sentences

The basic rule is simple. A sentence should have a clear subject and a clear verb.

Sentence Fragments

A sentence fragment is missing either a subject or verb.

> About three weeks ago at the Houston Astrodome, a couple of my friends, John and Eric, who were working there as hotdog vendors.

Run-on Sentences

A run-on sentence is composed of two independent sentences that are stuck together inappropriately.

> There were several baby gorillas at the zoo however the public wasn't allowed to see them yet.

Your Turn

11. Insert the missing periods in the paragraph below.

> Make sure you proofread your essay every writer commits errors in the first draft of an essay by proofreading what you wrote, you can catch and correct most or even all of your mistakes.

Note: Photocopying any part of this book is prohibited by law.

370

Vary Sentence Structure

To earn a high score on the essay, you'll need to go a bit beyond making sure that your sentences are punctuated correctly. You'll also need to vary the structure of your sentences.

Below is an example of the type of writing we want you to avoid.

> Falls are common in homes. They can cause injuries. They occur in bathrooms. They occur in the kitchen. They occur on stairs. They can occur almost anywhere. They can be prevented by cleaning up spills quickly. They can be prevented by using a step stool when you need to reach something in a high place.

Your Turn

12. How would you fix this paragraph?

_____

_____

_____

_____

Is That What You Meant To Say?

In high-pressure writing situations, many students write so quickly that they simply leave out punctuation marks and words. When you proofread, make sure you didn't leave anything out.

Your Turn

13. What's missing from the paragraph below?

In writing test, it's common students to skip over small words and punctuation marks We can all think quickly than we can write, so it's no surprise that this happens frequently. To make sure included every word and punctuation mark, reread each sentence slowly before you complete the essay portion the exam. You don't want confuse your readers by leaving something out just because you were in hurry.

Summary

In this unit, you learned that:

- the Standard Essay Template will help you write an effective essay.

- an introduction, at least two body paragraphs, and a conclusion are needed to make your essay complete.

- signal words let the reader know where you are going.

- good SAT essay style is concise, forceful, and creative.

- proofreading for common errors will improve your score.

Session 11: Practice Test #2

No material in this book.

Note: Photocopying any part of this book is prohibited by law.

375

Session 12: Test Review

In this unit, you will learn how to:

- check your test behavior against your pacing plan.

- improve your guessing.

- maximize your mental preparedness.

- evaluate your performance on each section of the test.

Note: Photocopying any part of this book is prohibited by law.

377

Why Do a Test Review?

There are a few very good reasons to spend the time looking at your performance on this test, including the following:

- While those exact questions won't be on your test, similar ones will be.

- Even though you are at the end of your course, you still have room for improvement, particularly in how you decide which questions to answer and how.

- The final practice test is a "dress rehearsal" for the SAT. By going over it now, you can be sure you won't make the same kinds of mistakes on Test Day.

Your Turn

How else could reviewing the final test help you on Test Day?

_____

_____

_____

Note: Photocopying any part of this book is prohibited by law.

378

The Test Review Approach

In this section, you'll

- focus on your process, not the score you got.

- reinforce everything you have learned during your SAT course.

- look at how you did on the test as a whole.

Why do you think your test-taking process is more important than the score you got on the practice test?

_____

_____

_____

Note: Photocopying any part of this book is prohibited by law.

379

Your Pacing Plan Revisited

How closely did you follow your pacing plan?

What You Planned to Do

Look back at your pacing plan. How many questions were you supposed to try in each section to meet your score goals?

Math: _____

Critical Reading: _____

Writing: _____

What You Actually Did

Now look at your final practice test. How many questions did you actually attempt in each section?

Math: _____

Critical Reading: _____

Writing: _____

Pacing Pitfalls

You probably didn't follow your pacing plan exactly. Here are three common pacing traps.

Running Out of Time

Did you run out of time in any sections? If so, why do you think that happened?

_____

_____

_____

Taking Too Long on Easy Questions

Did you take too long on any easier questions?

_____

_____

_____

Taking Too Long on Hard Questions

Did you spend too much time on any hard questions that you got wrong anyway?

_____

_____

_____

Pacing Pitfalls, Part II

Lack of confidence is a big problem for many SAT test-takers.

Changing Answers

Think about the questions that gave you trouble. How often did you change your initial answer to something else?

_____

_____

_____

How often did changing your answer help you? (In other words, how often did you change an incorrect answer to a correct answer?)

_____

_____

_____

Guessing

Remember the rules of SAT guessing:

- On multiple-choice questions, only guess if you can eliminate at least one answer choice with confidence.

- Always guess on Grid-Ins, which have no wrong answer penalty.

- Be cautious about guessing on the hardest questions in a set, as a seemingly wrong answer may not be.

Your Turn

What questions did you not know how to solve but could have guessed?

_____

_____

_____

What questions did you spend too much time trying to solve when you could have guessed?

_____

_____

_____

The Mental Game

The SAT can make you feel lots of different ways, from terrified to confident.

Your Turn

How did you feel while you were taking the practice test?

_____

_____

_____

Was the experience what you expected?

_____

_____

_____

What should you do if you see something unexpected on Test Day?

_____

_____

_____

Note: Photocopying any part of this book is prohibited by law.

384

The Mental Game, Part II

Another important part of the mental game is not letting the hard questions get the better of you.

Your Turn

Did you have any bad stretches of several questions in a row that you couldn't answer or got wrong? What do you think caused them?

_____

_____

_____

Were there some questions that you just couldn't get out of your mind? If so, what did you do?

_____

_____

_____

The Essay

Your Turn

Let's look at the important elements of your essay score individually.

Structure

How long was your essay?

_____

How many paragraphs did it have?

_____

Position

What was your position on the issue?

_____

_____

Evidence

What were the reasons you included to support your argument?

1. _____

2. _____

3. _____

Style

Did you write in complete sentences with proper spelling and punctuation?

_____

_____

Note: Photocopying any part of this book is prohibited by law.

386

Multiple-Choice Writing

During your course, you looked at the errors that most often show up in the multiple-choice Writing section. Let's see how they appeared in your practice test.

Your Turn

For each question from the practice test, identify the type of error present.

1. <u>The medicine community recognizes the negative effect of </u>magazine covers have on self-esteem, as advertising may contribute to fear of having "imperfect" skin and hair.

Error: _____

2. In the 1800s, most children <u>do not spend two decades of their life in school</u>; even by 1909, only 6 percent of all 17-year-olds became high-school graduates.

Error: _____

3. Temporary hearing loss or <u>ringing in the ears</u> is a regular occurrence
                                                A

<u>at concerts</u> where <u>they</u> sit or stand <u>next to</u> the gigantic speakers. <u>No error</u>
  B   C   D   E

Error: _____

4. <u>As I walked around, I have seen nothing</u> I considered to be art!

Error: _____

Wrong Answers in Multiple-Choice Writing

Common wrong answers in this section:
- correct one error but introduce another one
- correct one error but ignore another error in the same section
- correct the error but in a wordy way
- don't correct the error

Your Turn

Let's look at the choices for one of the questions from the previous page.

2. In the 1800s, most children <u>do not spend two decades of their life in school</u>; even by 1909, only 6 percent of all 17-year-olds became high-school graduates.

(A) do not spend two decades of their life in school
(B) don't spend two decades of their life in school
(C) do not spend two decades of their life going to school
(D) did not spend two decades of their lives in school
(E) did not spend two decades of their life in school

What makes each of the answers (other than D) wrong?

A. _____

B. _____

C. _____

E. _____

Sentence Completions: Sentence Types

Let's look at the common sentence types that showed up on your practice test.

Your Turn

For each question from the practice test, identify whether it is a Green Light, a U-Turn, or an S-Curve sentence.

1. Successful political candidates often start their campaigns a year before an election, thereby ------- voters to ------- the candidate's position on important issues.

Sentence type: _____

2. The performance by the unrehearsed student orchestra was truly a -------: every instrument clashed with the others in complete disharmony.

Sentence type: _____

3. While some members of the Thomas family ------- Uncle Joe for his repugnant social behavior, others tolerated his idiosyncrasies with the hopes of benefiting from the large estate that he was sure to leave behind when he died.

Sentence type: _____

4. Despite extensive evidence demonstrating the defendant's role in the forgery, the jury's perception of her ------- was minimized by her attorney's shrewd focus on her impressive history of charitable giving.

Sentence type: _____

Sentence Completions: Predictions

How well did you predict the blanks in Sentence Completions on your practice test?

Your Turn

For each question from the practice test, make a prediction for each blank.

1. The defending champion was an ------- athlete: no other contender had been able to equal his performance in the history of his career.

Prediction: _____

2. A leader may develop a flawless reputation by ------- irreproachable behavior, but then destroy his image by displaying -------.

Prediction 1:_____

Prediction 2:_____

3. The presenter turned out to be an ------- lecturer; his delivery was dull and lifeless, completely lacking vitality.

Prediction: _____

4. While trying to ------- a relationship with her new, quiet neighbor, Juanita mistakenly interpreted her neighbor's reserved behavior as ------- and started to avoid her instead.

Prediction 1:_____

Prediction 2:_____

Note: Photocopying any part of this book is prohibited by law.

390

Wrong Answers in Sentence Completions

The most common wrong answer type in Sentence Completions is Wrong Direction.

Your Turn

For each of the questions from the practice test, identify the wrong direction choice(s).

1. The rocking of the boat had ------- effect on the infant passengers in the boat's nursery: after two hours of exposure to the repetitive motion, most of the children fell asleep.

(A) a soporific
(B) an energizing
(C) an uninspiring
(D) a disheartening
(E) an enigmatic

Wrong Direction choice(s):

_____

_____

2. The performance by the unrehearsed student orchestra was truly a -------: every instrument clashed with the others in complete disharmony.

(A) triumph
(B) cacophony
(C) monotony
(D) euphony
(E) repetition

Wrong Direction choice(s):

_____

_____

Note: Photocopying any part of this book is prohibited by law.

391

Handling Reading Passages

Finding the important information in a passage is essential for answering the questions correctly.

Your Turn

Open your test booklet to Section 6, to the passage that accompanies questions 10-18. (This passage is about "film noir.") What is the main idea of each paragraph?

Paragraph 1: _____

_____

Paragraph 2: _____

_____

Paragraph 3: _____

_____

Paragraph 4: _____

_____

Paragraph 5: _____

_____

Paragraph 6: _____

_____

What is the main idea of the passage as a whole?

_____

_____

Note: Photocopying any part of this book is prohibited by law.

392

Reading Question Strategies

Your goal in reading the passages in the practice test was to answer the questions about them. Some questions are answered more easily than others, particularly if you are short on time.

Your Turn

For each question from the practice test, decide whether you could answer it quickly or not, and why.

1. As used in line 46, "secure" most nearly means

Quickly or not? _____

Why? _____

2. The information in the passage suggests that an attempt to reproduce a movie in the film noir genre today

Quickly or not? _____

Why? _____

3. According to the passage (lines 7-17), which of the following best describes how Americans perceived the transition they experienced after World War II?

Quickly or not? _____

Why? _____

4. Which statement best summarizes the author's views on the relationship between the genre of film noir and the social context within which it was developed?

Quickly or not? _____

Why? _____

Note: Photocopying any part of this book is prohibited by law.

393

Common Wrong Answers in Passage-Based Reading Questions

Common wrong answer types on Reading Comprehension include:
- outside the scope
- distortion choices
- opposite choices
- common meanings of words in Vocabulary-in-Context questions

Your Turn

For each question from the practice test, identify the common wrong answer choices it contains.

1. It can be inferred that the author of the passage believes that

A. dance should never be shown on television.
B. interest in dance is not likely to wane as a result of the public's fascination with television and movies.
C. dancers who perform on television are not as talented as those who perform on stage for a live audience.
D. the public is currently incapable of appreciating the depth and nuance of art forms such as dance.
E. the cultivation of popular tastes should be a primary concern of those working in the arts.

Common wrong answer choices: _____

_____

2. As used in line 46, "secure" most nearly means

(A) protect
(B) assign
(C) leave
(D) lock up
(E) obtain

Common wrong answer choices: _____

_____

Note: Photocopying any part of this book is prohibited by law.

394

Math Concepts

You spent several lessons looking at the concepts that most often show up in the Math sections. Let's see how they appeared in your practice test.

Your Turn

For each question from the practice test, identify the math concept being tested.

1. An industrious insect travels 1,680 feet per year. At this rate, how many months would it take for the insect to travel 560 feet?

Concept: _____

2. Which of the following is equal to $x^{\frac{3}{4}}$?

Concept: _____

3. If $2a - b = 7$ and $2a + 2b = 16$, what is the value of $3a + 7b$?

Concept: _____

4. For all integers k, let $* k *$ be defined as follows:

$* k * = 3k$ if k is positive.

$* k * = k^2 \div 3$ if k is negative.

If $* 1 * + * (-3) * = q$, what is the value of $2q^2$?

Concept: _____

Math Strategies

You also learned strategies to help you answer math questions quickly and efficiently.

Your Turn

For each question from the practice test, identify the type of strategy that would best help you answer the question.

1. If an integer, f, is divisible by 2, 4, 8, and 12, what is the next larger integer divisible by these numbers?

Strategy: _____

2. If c is 22 percent of e and d is 68 percent of e, what is $d - c$ in terms of e?

Strategy: _____

3. If y and z are positive integers, which of the following expressions is equivalent to $(5y)^z \times 5y$?

Strategy: _____

4. If $f(x) = 3x - 2$, for what value of x does $f(x)$ equal 1?

Strategy: _____

Wrong Answers in Math

Some of the most common wrong answer types in SAT Math include:

- clunkers
- rule breakers
- "obvious" choices

Your Turn

Identify the common wrong answer types in each of the following questions.

1. If $5 + k = 9$, what is the value of $5 \times k$?

(A) 4
(B) 20
(C) 45
(D) 70
(E) 81

Common wrong answer types:

_____

_____

2. If $3^d = 4,$ then $3^{3d} =$

(A) $\dfrac{4}{3}$
(B) 4
(C) 12
(D) 36
(E) 64

Common wrong answer types:

_____

_____

Note: Photocopying any part of this book is prohibited by law.

397

Summary

In this unit, you learned that:

- you will maximize your points by sticking to your pacing plan.

- you can eliminate common wrong answer choices to pick up points on questions that stump you.

- it's often better to guess on a question you're not sure about than to waste time trying to sort it out.

- by going through the errors you made under time pressure now, you'll be in great shape to avoid those mistakes on Test Day.

Session 12: Beating Test Stress

In this unit, you will learn to:

- desensitize yourself to stress by rehearsing the stressful event.

- focus on what you can control.

- maintain perspective.

- think positively.

- complete your preparation for the SAT.

Facts about Fear

If you are still feeling nervous, don't worry. It's normal to have some test anxiety.

You are not alone.

If you find yourself thinking, "I'm such a freak. No one else gets as nervous as I do," know that lots of people get nervous before exams, especially this kind of exam.

A little bit of stress can be good!

If you are an athlete, a musician, or any kind of performer, you know that nervous excitement can keep you energized and focused. Your goal is not to rid yourself of stress entirely. The key is keeping your stress at a manageable level.

You can do well even if you're afraid.

Many successful test takers experience test anxiety before and during exams. The key is not to react to that anxiety. Keep it at a manageable level.

Your fear does not reflect your ability or preparedness.

Some people get nervous even if they are very well prepared. Others don't get nervous, even when they should. There is no correlation between anxiety and your actual readiness for the exam.

Think of a time when you found nervous excitement to be helpful.

_____

Think of a time when you were nervous about something but did well.

_____

Stress Rehearsal

Studies have shown that rehearsing a stressful event can significantly reduce one's fear of that event. Stress rehearsals can be mental or physical. We recommend you do both.

You have already completed the most important part of your SAT rehearsal. You have been preparing for the exam by getting familiar with the test itself. As Test Day approaches, you can rehearse in other ways to keep your stress at bay.

Your Turn

What things can you do to reduce your stress before Test Day? Consider both physical and mental ways you can practice for the exam.

_____

_____

_____

_____

_____

_____

Note: Photocopying any part of this book is prohibited by law.

401

What Are You Afraid Of?

Rehearsing stressful events can help desensitize you to your anxiety; that is, while you may still feel anxious, it doesn't bother you as much. If you find yourself fearing the worst, desensitize yourself by imagining your worst-case scenario.

Your Turn

Make a list of everything that could possibly go wrong on Test Day.

_____

_____

_____

_____

_____

_____

Brainstorm solutions to things that could possibly go wrong.

_____

_____

_____

_____

_____

Note: Photocopying any part of this book is prohibited by law.

402

Worst-Case Scenarios

Here are some things that could go wrong on Test Day.

- You oversleep and miss your exam.
- Your car/bus breaks down on the way to the exam.
- You go to the wrong testing center.
- You forget to bring your ID and/or admission ticket.
- You forget your #2 pencil or your calculator.
- You get a Math section first, and you hate math.
- All your Reading Comprehension passages are horribly boring.
- Your mind goes blank while you are taking the test.
- You can't answer a single question because the test is in German.

Your Turn

Which of these things could actually happen?

_____

_____

_____

Which of these things are very unlikely to happen?

_____

_____

_____

Note: Photocopying any part of this book is prohibited by law.

403

When Things Go Wrong

Sometimes things do go wrong. What should you do?

You go to the wrong testing center.

If you arrive at the wrong testing center, you may be allowed to take the exam as a standby, though it's not guaranteed and costs more.

The best way to avoid this is: _____.

You forget your #2 pencil.

If you leave your #2 pencils at home, you can probably borrow a pencil from a fellow test taker or from the proctor.

The best way to avoid this is: _____.

You forget your calculator.

If you forget your calculator, you will not be able to borrow one. However, no math questions on the SAT require a calculator, so don't panic if you forget it.

The best way to avoid this is _____.

You get a math section first, and you hate math.

If you get your weakest subject first, at least you are getting it out of the way.

The best way to avoid this is: _____.

All your Reading Comprehension passages are horribly boring.

You don't need to be interested in the passage topics to do well on SAT Reading Comprehension.

The best way to avoid this is: _____.

Taking Control

An important stress buster is figuring out what you can control and what you can't. When you feel stressed, focus on factors that are within your control and ignore everything else. Fortunately, where the SAT is concerned, much lies within your control.

Your Turn

Make a list of those things about Test Day that you can control, and those that you can't.

Things you can control	Things you can't control

What's the best way to handle things that are out of your control?

_____

_____

_____

Brain Power

Focusing on things you can control means focusing on your own thoughts and behaviors. If you find yourself thinking negatively during the test:

Notice It

Notice your thoughts. Some of them will be dull. You will think about the weather and what you had for breakfast. Notice that part of you is thinking and part of you is observing what you're thinking.

Label It

Say you see the first question and think: "All those sentences look right to me. I'm so bad at grammar." Part of you is panicking about grammar and part of you is observing you panicking. Use the part of you that is observing to label those thoughts as destructive.

Breathe

Your heart might be beating faster than usual. If so, take a moment to breathe. Ten slow, deep breaths will lower your heart rate immediately.

Let It Go

Once you have taken a deep breath, try releasing the negative thought.
- Think the word "stop."
- Use images. Picture the thought inside a thought bubble, and then picture the thought bubble floating away.
- Tell the thought: "Thanks for warning me, but I'm going to let you go now."

Talk Back

For persistent negative thoughts, you may need to talk back. You might say to yourself: "OK, so it's grammar. It isn't my favorite, but I'm not giving up." Even the smallest challenge is usually enough to help you regain your equilibrium.

Note: Photocopying any part of this book is prohibited by law.

406

Positive Thinking

The mind is highly suggestible. As you get ready to take the test, remember to take care of your brain. After all, it has been working overtime for you.

- Pat yourself on the back for all your hard work.
- Set yourself up for success with a good night's sleep.
- Focus on your strengths as you go into the test.
- Tell yourself that you can do well on standardized tests.
- Stay in the game, even when you get those tough questions.
- _____
- _____

If you tell yourself you're going to suffer for the entire test, your mind will believe you and will get ready to suffer. If you tell yourself that you are a pretty good person who deserves to do well, your mind will believe you and will get ready to perform to the best of its ability!

Mantras

Mantras are phrases people repeat to themselves to help train their minds. Think of a mantra you can use to stay positive.

_____

_____

Note: Photocopying any part of this book is prohibited by law.

407

Be Prepared

Coming into the home stretch, here's what you need to do.

Know the Test

Review the directions for all question types, so you won't need to take valuable time to reread them during the exam.

Question types to review: _____

Know the Content

Focus on remembering what you have already learned, and let go of the rest.

Best question areas: _____

Know the Strategies

Review the strategies, so they will be at your fingertips on Test Day.

Strategies to review:

_____

Practice

The closer you get to the exam date, the more you should work with test-like questions under simulated test-like conditions.

Date to take a practice test: _____

Have the Right Attitude

Think positively and focus on remaining calm so you can access what you know on Test Day.

Strategy to stay calm: _____

If You Haven't Improved

Thinking positively is all well and good, but what if you really haven't improved from when you started the course?

Cut Your Losses

Once you have studied as hard as you can, give yourself a break in your weak areas. You can miss some questions and still do well on the SAT as a whole.

Focus on Your Strengths

In the final days before the exam, build your confidence by focusing on and reinforcing your strong areas.

Be Skeptical

If you feel you haven't improved, you may be wrong. It may be test stress talking.

Consider Your Options

You can always retake the SAT. If you're sure you did terribly when you come out of the exam, you can have your test thrown out before it's scored.

Cancellation Is a Last Resort

If it's absolutely necessary, you can postpone your test and take it the next time it is offered. Will you really use the time to study, though, or will you just worry?

Summary

In this unit, you learned that:

- rehearsing stressful events can help desensitize you to anxiety.

- imagining your worst-case scenario can help you strategize solutions to possible mishaps.

- focusing on what you can control is the secret to doing well.

- thinking positively can help your performance on Test Day.

- you should adopt a mental attitude geared for success.

Note: Photocopying any part of this book is prohibited by law.

410

Session 12: Last-Minute Advice

In this unit, you will learn to:

- set yourself up for success the night before the test.

- get into the right frame of mind on the morning of the test.

- stay calm, cool, and collected during the test.

- make the most of your break time.

- reclaim your life after the test.

The Night before the Test

The night before the test, relax your mind and body. Cramming doesn't work and could undermine the preparation you've already done. The night before the SAT:

Do	Don't
<ul><li>Get a good night's sleep.</li><li>Lay out the things you need for the next day.</li><li>Arrange for a backup wake-up call.</li><li>Check your admission ticket for the address of the testing center.</li><li>Have some fun, but not too much fun.</li></ul>	<ul><li>Try to learn any new material.</li><li>Review and drill late into the night.</li><li>Talk about the test, if you can help it.</li><li>Make any big life decisions or get into arguments.</li><li>Drink too much caffeine.</li></ul>

List three things you could do the night before the test that would be "some fun, but not too much fun."

1. _____

2. _____

3. _____

Why shouldn't you make life decisions or get into arguments the night before the test?

_____

Pack Your Bag

Pack your bag the night before so you won't have to think about it in the morning. Remember to include:

- Admission ticket
- Acceptable photo ID
- Sharpened #2 pencils
- Calculator with fresh batteries
- Snacks for the breaks
- Sweater
- Watch

What qualifies as acceptable ID?

_____

_____

_____

What else might you want or need on the day of the test? Write down those things now so that you remember them when you pack your bag.

_____

_____

_____

The Morning of the Test

Make sure your body has everything it needs to perform well.

Do	Don't
<ul><li>Eat a light and nutritious breakfast.</li><li>Drink enough water.</li><li>Dress in layers.</li><li>Arrive 15-30 minutes early.</li></ul>	<ul><li>Have too much caffeine.</li><li>Run through your flash cards.</li><li>Socialize before the test starts.</li><li>Bring food or drink into the testing room.</li><li>Be late.</li></ul>

Why shouldn't you socialize with other test takers before the test starts?

_____

_____

_____

Plan what you will eat for breakfast on the morning of the exam:

_____

_____

_____

During the Test

To have a successful testing experience, you will need to manage your time well.

Pacing

By now, you should know how many questions you need to answer correctly to achieve your target score. Stick to your plan. Don't be afraid to skip questions just because this is the "real thing."

Slow and Steady

Don't rush and don't get bogged down in one killer question. Remember, you get the same number of points for easy questions as you do for hard questions.

Use Your Time

If you finish early, see if you can eliminate wrong answer choices on any questions you left blank, and check answers to questions you were unsure of. At the end of each section, check that you filled in each circle completely and that you fully erased any answer that you changed.

Breathe

If your mind goes blank, stop working and take a few moments to breathe. You are under a time pressure, but taking a moment to collect your thoughts is good time management.

Remember your Mantra

In Beating Test Stress, you came up with a mantra that you can say to yourself if you're starting to get anxious. Do you remember what it was? Have you been using it? Write down your mantra (or come up with a new one) here:

_____

_____

Note: Photocopying any part of this book is prohibited by law.

415

Test Etiquette

Be a polite test taker. Your proctor will go over the rules of your testing center. A few general rules for all testing centers include the following:

Do	Don't
<ul><li>Fill out student information carefully.</li><li>Use the answer grid.</li><li>Request the proctor's permission to move your seat if someone is disturbing you.</li><li>Return to the room on time after breaks.</li></ul>	<ul><li>Talk to fellow test takers during the test for any reason.</li><li>Operate any electrical device other than your calculator.</li><li>Jump ahead in your testing booklet to another section.</li><li>Eat or drink in the testing room.</li><li>Make any unnecessary noise.</li></ul>

What is the best way to handle a disruptive test taker?

_____

_____

What will happen if you jump ahead to another section in your testing booklet?

_____

_____

Note: Photocopying any part of this book is prohibited by law.

416

Avoid Common Pitfalls

During the test, avoid these common pitfalls:

Don't read hidden meanings into patterns of answer choices.

Why?

_____

_____

Don't assume the section is experimental.

Why?

_____

_____

Don't guess randomly.

Why?

_____

_____

Don't give up.

Why?

_____

_____

Don't be distracted if you think you see an error.

Why?

_____

_____

During the Breaks

During the breaks:

Do	Don't
<ul><li>Keep to yourself.</li><li>Have a light snack.</li><li>Stretch your legs.</li><li>Visit the restroom, if necessary.</li><li>Stay close by.</li></ul>	<ul><li>Talk to other test takers.</li><li>Review flash cards.</li><li>Wander away from the testing center.</li><li>Return late.</li></ul>

What are some good snacks to bring for the breaks?

_____

_____

Why shouldn't you talk to other test takers during the breaks?

_____

_____

Use All of Your Time

If you finish a section early, go back to the questions you left blank and see if you can eliminate any wrong answer choices.

Your Turn

Number the steps in the order in which you should complete them.

_____ Go back and attack the hardest questions.
_____ Check to see that you completely filled in your answers on the grid.
_____ Answer as many easier questions as you can.
_____ Return to harder questions to see if you can eliminate anything and guess.

Retaking the Test

What if, after all your effort, you aren't happy with your performance on Test Day?

You can take the test again.

There is no guarantee you will do better the second time, but if you truly feel you could have done better, you can always retake the test.

How should you decide whether to retake the SAT?

_____

_____

You can cancel your score.

You can cancel your score immediately after the exam up to the Wednesday following the exam. Your entire score will be erased from all records.

Why might you NOT want to cancel your score, even if you think you did poorly?

_____

_____

Note: Photocopying any part of this book is prohibited by law.

419

You're Done!

After the test, congratulate yourself on a job well done.

What you should do after the test:

_____

_____

What you shouldn't do after the test:

_____

_____

Your Score Report

Your score report is added to the computer files within three weeks after your test date, at which point it is mailed to you. You can also access your scores online or by phone (for an additional fee) two weeks after your exam date.

Do you think you will want to find out your scores early? Why or why not?

_____

_____

Summary

In this unit, you learned that:

- you shouldn't panic the night before the exam.

- you should bring all the right materials to the test.

- you should always practice good test-taking etiquette.

- you should manage your time during the test.

- you should relax directly following the test.